Using Math to Calm Students During Learning for Non-Speaking and Unreliable Verbal Individuals:

Lessons for Soma®RPM and Other Choice Based Systems

By: Lenae Crandall

GW00455046

Using Math to Calm Students During Learning for Non-Speaking and Unreliable Verbal Individuals: Lessons for Soma®RPM and Other Choice Based Systems

By: Lenae Crandall

Acknowledgements:

Thank you to Soma Mukhopadhyay for letting me learn from you and for feedback on portions of this book.

Thanks to the students, parents and other professionals who support and encourage me and whom I learn from.

Introduction:

Some students get up in the air during Rapid Prompting Method (RPM) sessions or during learning with any methodology. A topic may trigger emotional outburst. Students may come to a learning session already up in the air. They may cry, laugh, pull hair, pinch, bite, scratch, self-injury, destroy objects, hit or bite tables, bounce and noise make, and get into a variety of excitatory stims. These are often instinctual actions.

Teachers wonder, "what is wrong?" or "is she hurting?" or "does he did like me?" etc. Sometimes a little bit of math calms the student right down and helps the student regulate. In chapter 16, page 214, of *Understanding Autism Through Rapid Prompting Method*, (2008) Soma Mukhopadhyay discusses ways to calm an excited student doing instinctual actions. Soma, (pg. 211) defines instinctual actions as those actions done impulsively such as grabbing food or hair. When students get in these excitatory states, sometimes doing parallel math, poetry or stories in the lesson will help the student regulate and make for a successful session. (pg. 214)

In my experience, students calm with math in different ways. Sometimes math is like magic and student immediately calm once I start or sometimes when I even suggest math. Other times math slowly works it magic. With some students, stories or poetry are a better way to calm or a mixture of a couple of these along with other techniques that are part of RPM (some listed on page 214 in Soma's book listed above.).

With some students, it is best to do unrelated math problems to the lesson I am doing. Sometimes it is best to let the student make up and solve their own math problems for a bit. Others, I need to connect the math to the lesson itself. With some, I find it best to do math and then lead into a topic—picking up the math again here and there after that in the lessons. In RPM, we individualize and here is no exception.

In this book, I have written twenty-one lessons with math weaved into each lesson in a variety of ways. You may need to adapt to the student as timing the math can be critical. Some will benefit from doing math problems for a longer amount of time. Some will need different types of math problems to solve. You may need to break down the math problems more to help the student solve them. While a few new math concepts are taught. In most cases, it is assumed the student has already been taught the math as they typically involve math problems with + ,-.x,÷. Review the lessons before-hand and prepare to teach the math, if needed, or change the math problems to something they already know or more appropriate for their age.

The goal of this book is to help you see how you can weave math into lessons and figure out which way works best to calm and regulate the student(s) you work with.

While this book was written for Soma®RPM (a teaching method that empowers the learner to communicate as well as learn functional skills and hobbies), those using choice based systems in general may find them useful. I hope these lessons helpful on your journey!

Sincerely,

Lenae Crandall
Certified Soma®RPM Provider

HOW TO USE THIS BOOK

Understanding Lessons

Here is what a lesson looks like without my commentary on how to use it:

LESSON 1: HOW PLANTS GROW (CHILD)

> **Main Cognitive Objective(s):** Students will acquire knowledge and gain understanding of how plants grow.
>
> **Application of Math:** Applied directly to the lesson--counting
>
> **Materials:** small box of crayons or markers with basic colors.

STATE: Let's see. . . how will we get a <u>plant</u> to grow! First we need a tiny <u>seed</u>. (*fold up a tiny corner of paper into a seed*)

ASK: To get a plant to grow, we need a (SEED. or VAN)?

EXPAND: And something else small like a seed could be a (CAT or PEA.)?
"Peas can be tiny as a seed, but you know, some seeds are even smaller."
MATH: And let's count seeds. Here I have some seeds (*draw 3 seeds then tap each*). So how many seeds to I have? (3. or 5)?
"Yes, that is 3 seeds!"
MATH: And what if I had 2 more? (*draw 2 more and tap all five*) Count them and now how many do I have? (5. or 8)?
"Yes, 5 seeds!"

Below is a sample lesson again with my commentary on how to use it. *In this font,* I will indicate how to read these lessons:

In bold at the top is the lesson number and concept being taught.

LESSON 1: HOW PLANTS GROW (CHILD)

> **Main Cognitive Objective(s):** Students will acquire knowledge and gain understanding of how plants grow.
> *Application...Tells how Math will be used in the lesson.*
> **Application of Math:** Applied directly to the lesson--counting
>
> **Materials:** small box of crayons or markers with basic colors.
> *These are the materials needed in addition to your paper, tape, pencils, letter-boards, stencils, etc.*

STATE: Let's see. . . how will we get a <u>plant</u> to grow! First we need a tiny <u>seed</u>. (*fold up a tiny corner of paper into a seed*)

'ASK' questions check for listening and help you as the teacher, check your technique. The capital letters are the two choices to give the students (if they need or are using choices). The answer with a period. is the correct answer.

ASK: To get a plant to grow, we need a (SEED. or VAN)?

"EXPAND' these are thinking questions where learners communicate connections, reasoning, opinions, thoughts, etc. Capital letters are the choices if needed. The answer with the period is the correct answer. If there is not period, then it is an opinion questions and any choice can be correct. Students who are able to generate their own responses by spelling don't need to use choices each time.

EXPAND: And something else small like a seed could be a (CAT or PEA.)?

The gray letters in italics are suggested words to say that give more information, confirm information, and make the lesson a discussion. RPM should not be a list of questions, but balanced between teacher and student performance.

"Peas can be tiny as a seed, but you know, some seeds are even smaller."

MATH: And let's count seeds. Here I have some seeds (*draw 3 seeds then tap each*). So how many seeds to I have? (3. or 5)?

"Yes, that is 3 seeds!"

MATH: And what if I had 2 more? (*draw 2 more and tap all five*) Count them and now how many do I have? (5. or 8)?

"Yes, 5 seeds!"

To help with implementing lessons, it might be helpful to review lessons by high lighting the STATE sections in a color (like red), the ASK questions a different color (like blue) and the expand questions in a different color (like yellow). This way as you reference the lesson your eyes will have an easier time finding the lesson point you are on, without slowing down and losing the student's interest. This may be particularly helpful if the student you are working with is a mover. You may need to carry the lesson, paper, pencils, etc., around with you until you can help the student find a more stationary place. This regulation may take time.

You might write in notes with a pencil to indicate how you might individualize for a student. For example, if the student needs a bit shorter amount of information given in the STATE section, draw a line in the sentence where you will pause to ask a question. Then, you might add an arrow from the break to the question or write in of that question. You might write in alternate choices or rephrase a question to make it more conducive for open ended communication to happen for students who are ready. Little changes and adaptations can make a big difference in how successful the lesson turns out. Visit this link to understand more about implementing lessons: https://www.youtube.com/watch?v=EfOrTWteI1Q&t=117s

Choices and Student Responses (*See chapter 12 of "Understanding Autism Using Rapid Prompting Method" by Soma Mukhopadhyay (2008)*)

FOR Soma®RPM: Choices are spelled out and written in front of the student. They are placed equal distance to the choosing hand. We either rip paper choices into two pieces or hold up a folded piece of paper with the choices written on it. Here are two example videos: https://youtu.be/-D28Zl3ZUsU and https://www.youtube.com/edit?o=U&video_id=CtLfkXaSHak.

Choices should be written left to right as you read in the order you write and say them. The correct answer, however, will not always be first. That should vary.

NOT all students will begin with the paper choices. Some will do choices directly on the alphabet stencils, number stencils, or laminated letter/number board.

Some will get to a point that for a number of questions you will not need choices, but can ask the question and then present the letter/number board or stencils and the student can respond without a choice.

Some will be ready to generate their own words, phrases or sentences. You can add to the questions or change the questions to encourage more responses from the student.
FOR THOSE USING OTHER RESPONSE SYSTEMS OR METHODS: The choices are written down for you to use. You can program a device, use switches, write on a white board, or use paper as in RPM. Follow the system you use to adapt lessons accordingly.

Ways to Handle Incorrect Responses

If a student doesn't correctly choose, there are a number of things you can do. After first, or if it is evident the student is teasing or anxious, instead of telling the student they are wrong, you would make light of it or twist it into the correct answer. For example, if I state and ask, "The triangle has three sides. How many sides does a triangle have? (3. or 4)?" and the student picks 4, you could say, "Oh, you want the triangle to be a square. Maybe you are against triangles today."

If the student keeps picking one side, then sometimes you put a weird answer like a wiggly line to "wake up" the student on the side the student keeps picking. The other side will have the correct answer.

If the student just randomly hits, you can refrain from paper choices and put tape on two numbers or two letters for the response.

Another way to help a student reason and focus is to give a correct choice and then a very long unfamiliar word. For example, "When we begin counting objects, we start with number 1. What number do we start with? (SPANISH EQUITY or 1.)?"

When the concept is new, it can be appropriate to reteach, unless it seems the miss wasn't due to lack of understanding. THOSE USING OTHER METHODS may always reteach, like this: "After 2 comes 3. What will come after 3? (4. or 0)?" Student touches 0. "Listen, 1,2,3,4. 4 comes after 3. What comes after three? (4. or 0)?"

There are more ways to handle incorrect responses. What we don't say is "try again" or "no, wrong again!" and make a student feel bad about themselves.

Sensory Activities

Sensory activities are writing the key words, drawing, ripping the paper (for choices), making models and other things you do to stimulate the different senses of the student to help learning take place. These are embedded in the lessons (or if not written in the lesson, how you will implement these lessons if you are doing Soma®RPM), but part of adapting to the individual student may be to add more, subtract a few, or change them up. At times, I have given suggestions at the top of the lesson or throughout the lesson for sensory activities.

Adaptation and Personalizing

If using this book in conjunction with Soma®RPM, you will want to adapt and personalize. Each student is an individual with a unique sensory system, personality, preferences and so forth. As such, writing lessons for the masses proves tricky. As a teacher, you will need to pre-read lessons and adapt accordingly. I provide 2 choices for pretty much every question. Some students will not need the choices or can choose from more than two choices. Some can generate their own responses. A student who has just begun may be very nervous and reasoning between choices may increase anxiety, so for a few lessons you might not even use choices, but directly move to spelling or touching numbers on the stencil/ laminated number board.

Some students have unique family circumstances, life experiences and so forth. As a result, some stories, lessons, or questions may need to adapt to that student's individual circumstances.

Some students will need a faster pace of back and forth between teacher and student. You will intersperse questions throughout the 'STATE' section (Discussed below), rather than teach the sentence or two before discussion, as it is written. If you do not, you might lose the student's interest and the lesson fall apart.

Some students need fast pace, some need a quiet voice, some need more auditory, some need more visual, some need more tactile or kinesthetic activities. To implement best practice Soma®RPM, you will need to adapt to these in the instance of learning.

Lessons and Content

There are a variety of topics presented in these lessons. Each lesson has math interweaved into it to help calm and regulate a student. These are meant to give you ideas of how to use the math to calm and regulate a student. It is assumed the student has previously been taught the math in most cases. Therefore, you'll want to review the lessons and plan to teach the math if the student hasn't been taught OR change to concepts the student has been taught. As the teacher, you have to decide if the student needs more math problems in a row, less often, or more frequently. Some lessons are more appropriate for older students and some more appropriate for younger students. Adapt according to the student's age.

You'll find some lessons are better for calming an already up in the air student and some lessons are better for keeping a student regulated throughout the lesson, so they will not get more dysregulated and can calm down to make the learning teaching experience better for everyone.

Objectives

A proper Soma®RPM lesson has four goals:
1- Education/Cognitive Goals
2- Skill Goals
3- Tolerance Goals
4- Communication Goals

The Education goals are topics for children and up.

The skill goals are the words students spell in the lesson after they choose, or when the student generates a response. Other skill goals are in the motor movements learned such as learning 'how' and 'what' to choose. They may also be the motor skills, taught in the motor skills lessons.

Tolerance goals are individualized to the student. They could be things such as tolerate the teacher's voice, length of time for the lesson, holding the pencil to point, tolerating the topics, fluency of spelling (also a skill goal) and more. Regulating their body.

Communication goals are answers to the questions and participation in discussion. They include fact, reasoning, thoughts, opinions, and discussion. Some students will do so in choices, some in a word, phrase, or sentence spelled.

In each of these 4 goals, the objectives are individualized, therefore I have not felt it necessary to specify what they are in each lesson.

Materials

For each lesson, you will need: paper, pencil, clear tape, timer (to show the student how long the session will be), stencils (letters and numbers) or laminated letter/number board. Additional materials are listed at the top of each lesson. Those using other systems will just need paper, pencils, clear tape, timer, and any other materials unique to the student.

Closing Lessons

In Soma®RPM we typically just close a discussion naturally. In typical special education instruction, teachers usually complement the student on their performance and behavior. Then, they let the student know what will be taught next. This is all good to do. Those doing Soma®RPM should not be hyper-focusing on "good boy/girl" or "bad boy/girl" for each lesson or giving insincere complements. Learning is the reward. Teachers should acknowledge trying and give calming feedback when students mess up, "Oops, just one letter off, no big deal" or "I can see you meant to touch that one."

LESSON 1: HOW PLANTS GROW (CHILD)

Main Cognitive Objective(s): Students will acquire knowledge and gain understanding of how plants grow.

Application of Math: math connect to the lesson--counting

Materials: small box of crayons or markers with basic colors.

STATE: Let's see. . . how will we get a <u>plant</u> to grow! First we need a tiny <u>seed</u>. (*fold up a tiny corner of paper into a seed*)

ASK: To get a plant to grow, we need a (SEED. or VAN)?

EXPAND: And something else small like a seed could be a (CAT or PEA.)?
"Peas can be tiny as a seed, but you know, some seeds are even smaller."
MATH: And let's count seeds. Here I have some seeds (*draw 3 seeds then tap each*). So how many seeds to I have? (3. or 5)?
"Yes, that is 3 seeds!"
MATH: And what if I had 2 more? (*draw 2 more and tap all five*) Count them and now how many do I have? (5. or 8)?
"Yes, 5 seeds!"

STATE: We will <u>dig</u> (*rip a tiny hole in the center of the paper*) a little hole in the <u>soil</u> (*color with brown crayon around the hole*) and put the seed inside it. (*put the seed inside the hole*)

ASK: We (DIG. or KICK OPEN) a hole?

EXPAND: And we dig with our (NOSE or SHOVEL.)?
"Yes, probably with a small shovel!"
MATH: Oh! And how many holes do we have here! (*draw 4 holes and tap each*) We have (5 or 4.)?
"Yes! we have 4 holes!"
MATH: And we have 4 more holes. (*draw 4 more*) Now count them (*tap all 8 holes*) and we have? (7 or 8.)?
"Now we have 8, yes!"

STATE: We put a little <u>water</u> (*take blue and put 6 dots on the soil-student can help*) with the seed and cover it with soil. (*tape the hole up or cover it with the ripped-out piece of paper*)

ASK: And what did we put on the seed to help it grow? (WATER. or FRUIT PUNCH)?

MATH: Let's see if we can count the dots of water we put on our seed? (*Tap each dot*) (6. or 7) drops of water?

STATE: Then we <u>wait</u>, and wait, and wait, and wait for it to grow.

ASK: And what do we do while the plant grows? (JUMP or WAIT.)?

MATH: Waiting can be hard! I am going to put a line for each hour I have waited for my plant to grow. (*draw 7 lines*) How many hours have I waited? (*tap each line for the student to count*) (5 or 7.)?
"Yes, 7 hours and I am sure there will be more."
EXPAND: Do you think it is hard to wait? (YES or NO)?
Comment on student response.

STATE: We water it each day (*put dots of blue water with crayon on it again*) and make sure it gets plenty of <u>sun</u>light. (*draw a sun*)

ASK: Oh! So, what do we need to get this plant to grow? Make sure it gets (COLD or SUN.) light?

EXPAND: Do you (LIKE or DISLIKE) the sun?
Comment on the student's response.
MATH: What if we have more than 1 sun! (*draw 9 suns*) How many suns did I draw (*tap each sun for the student to count*) (9. or 10) suns?
"We have 9 suns! Wow! The world would be super-hot!"

STATE: <u>Roots</u> grow from the seed into the ground. (*draw the outline of the seed over its location on the paper and then with pencil draw roots going into the soil.*)

ASK: So, we have what that grows into the ground? (FEET or ROOTS.)?

EXPAND: Do you think the roots help it to (SWING or STAY.) in one spot?
"Yes, and roots also is where the water goes into the plant."
MATH: Let's count the number of strings from the root. (*tap each strand of root*) How many do we have? (*give two choices- one correct and one incorrect*)

STATE: A tiny <u>bud</u> starts to <u>sprout</u> from the ground above the soil. (*draw a small bud sprouting- you can also draw and tape one on it*)

ASK: A tiny (FOOT or BUD.) begins to sprout?

EXPAND: And do you think sprout means to begin to (GROW. or EAT)?

MATH: Let's see if we can count these other buds (*draw 2 buds...tap each bud*) How many buds do we have? (2. or 5)?

MATH: And now we will add 4 more. (*draw 4 more...tap each bud*) How many do we have now? (6. or 8)?

STATE: Then out will grow the <u>stem</u> (*draw a longer stem*) with leaves (*draw leaves*) and then a <u>flower</u> on top. (*draw a flower on top*)

ASK: When it goes, there will be a (FLOWER. or POT) on top?

EXPAND: A stem is (SHORT or LONG.) compared to a flower?
"Yes, long, usually."
MATH: Let's count these lines and pretend they are stems (*draw 3 lines and tap each for the student to count*) How many stems? (4 or 3.)?

MATH: Now how many if I draw 5 more? (8. or 9)?

STATE: Plants need sunlight, water, and soil to <u>grow</u>.

ASK: Plants need sunlight, water and soil to (WIN or GROW.)?

EXPAND: What else grows? (PEOPLE. or TOYS)? And what else? (CARS or ANIMALS.)?

EXPAND: Let's name an animal that would grow? Do you want to say (ROSE or DOG.)?

MATH: Let's say we have these dogs (*draw 2*) How many dogs do we have? (2. or 3)?

EXPANSION ACTIVITY: Review the how a plant grows with questions like:
What do we need first for a plant to grow?
And after we dig the hole what do we put inside it?
We need to water it and cover the hole with?
Then we have to...

LESSON 2: STORY OF LUCY (CHILD)

Main Cognitive Objective(s): Students will acquire knowledge and gain understanding of appropriate ways to ask for thing through a story.

Application of Math: Math interspersed unrelated to the content of the lesson—Skip Counting

Materials:
*before you teach the lesson, look at the bold 'EXPAND' word on the second page at the bottom and come up with other options

---

STATE: Lucy (*do a simple drawing of a girl*) went outside to eat her carrots and <u>crackers</u>. (*draw crackers*) A <u>dog</u> (*draw a paper dog and have it run by Lucy*) came by and snatched her crackers out of her hand and ran away!

ASK: Lucy is eating carrots and (PEAS or CRACKERS.)? And who took the crackers from her? (DOG. or BROTHER)?

MATH: Let's skip count by 2's: 2, 4, 6, and (8. or 13)? 10, 12, 14, 16, 18, and (19 or 20.)? Then 22, 24, then (26. or 27)? 28, 30... (*keep going if the student still isn't calm*)

STATE: Lucy began to cry and cry, until the <u>ground</u> around her was covered in water!

ASK: What was covered in water after she cried for a while? (GROUND. or HANDS)?

EXPAND: Do you think someone could really cry that much? (YES or NO.)?
Comment on student's response.
MATH: Now, we'll skip count some more, but by 3's. 3, 6, and (12 or 9.)? Then 12, 15, And (18. or 20)? 21, 24, 27, 30, Then (31 or 33.)? ...(*keep going if the student still isn't calm*)

STATE: She just kept on crying because now she was <u>stuck</u> crying. The water rose to her <u>ankles</u>, (*draw a water line by her ankles*) but Lucy just kept crying and crying! Suddenly the water was to her <u>knees</u>. (*draw a water line by her knees*)

ASK: She kept on crying because now she is (STUCK. or COLD) crying?
"Yeah, she is crying so much she forgot how to stop. I wonder if she ever will!"
SPELL: Let's spell ANKLES and KNEES.

EXPAND: Wow! Lucy must drink a lot of water! What do you think? Do you (AGREE or DISAGREE)?

MATH: And let's skip count by 4's. 4, 8, 12, Then (13 or 16.) and 20, 24 and (28. or 30)? Then 32, 26, 40, 44, 48 and (49 or 52.)? . . . (*continue skip counting if the student isn't calm*)

STATE: But, that didn't stop her <u>tears</u>. She cried until the water was up to her <u>waste</u>. (*draw water to her waste*)

ASK: Even though it got to her knees, it didn't stop her (SMILE or TEARS.)?

EXPAND: Does this mean she didn't stop (RIPPING PAPER or CRYING.)?
"Yes, we often have tears when we cry."
SPELL: Spell WASTE.

MATH: Let's skip count by 5's. You start? (5. or 8)? 5, 10, 15, 20 then, (25. or 21)? 30, 35, 40, 45 and (46 o 50.)? Then 55, 60, 65 and (70. or 80)?... (*keep going if the student is still up in the air*)

STATE: Finally, her <u>dad</u> came out and said, "Lucy, what is going on?" Lucy cried louder, then said through tears, "A dog took my crackers!"

ASK: Who came out to ask why she was crying? (DAD. or MOM)?

EXPAND: Did Lucy tell? (YES. or NO)?

MATH: Let's skip count by 10's. 10, then (30 or 20.)? 30, 40 then (50. or 70)?... (*Keep going if student is still up in the air*)

STATE: Her dad said, "Lucy, why didn't you just <u>ask</u> for more crackers?" "Oh," Lucy said, "I guess I could have."

ASK: What could Lucy done instead of cry? (ASK. or HOPE) for more crackers?

EXPAND: So, if you have some problem, you can (READ or ASK.) for help?

EXPAND: Should we ask by (HITTING or (*give a way based off student's abilities that they could ask*).)?
Comment on student response.
MATH: Figure out what I am skip counting by and tell me what comes next. 2, 4, 6, 8. Am I counting by (TWOS. or FIVES)? What comes next? (10. or 11)?...(*Continue with math as needed*)
"Now, back to our story!"

STATE: With that, Lucy <u>stopped</u> crying, <u>waded</u> through the water to get inside, and asked, "<u>May</u> I have more crackers?"

ASK: She stops crying and then she (WADED. or WATCHED) in the water?

EXPAND: Do you think waded means, (WALKED. or RAN) through the water?
"Yes, she goes through the water and ask some questions."
EXPAND: Do you think that Lucy should have asked for more crackers (BEFORE. or AFTER) crying?
Comment on student response.
MATH: Ok, what am I skip counting by now? 5, 10, 15, 20, 25, and...by (FIVES. or TENS)? What comes next? (20 or 30.)? . . . (*keep going as needed*)

STATE: Here dad gave her some and that was that. Lucy went to the <u>window</u> to eat her crackers and carrots as she watched the water go down outside.

ASK: Where does Lucy sit this time, to eat her crackers? (STAIRS or WINDOW.)?

EXPAND: Where do you think the water will go? Through the (GROUND. or INTO FENCES)?

EXTENSION ACTIVITY: Have the student practice asking for something they need or want. Explain that sometimes what we want, we don't always get right then. Talk about how others also have a say in what happens, etc.

LESSON 3: VIKINGS

Main Cognitive Objective(s): Students will acquire knowledge and gain understanding of basic Viking facts.

Application of Math: Began with math and lead into the lesson

Materials:

STATE: Let's say your mom went out and collected <u>10 berries</u> and then picked <u>5 more</u>. How many berries would she have?

ASK: What are we pretending your mom collect? (FEATHERS or BERRIES.)?

EXPAND: And 10+5= (15. or 17)?

STATE: Let's say the next day, your grandma went out and collected <u>5 mushrooms</u> and then later on in the day collected <u>7</u> more. How many mushrooms would you have altogether?

ASK: What did your grandma collect? (MUSHROOMS. or FINS)?

EXPAND: And 5+7 mushrooms equals (12. or 13)?

STATE: Now let's say that you ate <u>6</u> of the 15 berries your mom collect. How many are left?

ASK: So, what do you do with 6 of the berries? (FINISHED or ATE.) them?

EXPAND: And how many are left? (10 or 9.)?

STATE: What if <u>3</u> of your grandma's 12 mushrooms were not good and you threw them out. How many would she have left?

ASK: So, some of the mushrooms were (RED or BAD.) did we say?

EXPAND: And 12-3 equals? (9. or 8)?

STATE: Do you know that long ago <u>Vikings</u> lived. The <u>women</u> collected mushrooms and berries.

ASK: Who are we talking about? (FRIENDS or VIKINGS.)?

ASK: And who collected the berries? (WOMEN. or MEN)?

EXPAND: Would you want to collect berries or mushrooms? (YES or NO)?
Comment on student's response.

STATE: Now, Viking men went <u>hunting</u> for food.

ASK: What did Viking men do? (HUNT. or DESTROY) food?

EXPAND: What are some animals one might hunt? Do you think (BEARS. or LADYBUGS)?
Comment on student's response.

STATE: Let's say a Viking caught <u>3 bears</u> one day and <u>2</u> bears the next. How many bears did he catch?

ASK: What did he catch? (BEARS. or WOLVES)?

EXPAND: And how many did he catch? (4 or 5.)?

STATE: The Vikings also did a lot of <u>farming</u>.

ASK: What did the Vikings do a lot of? (PARADING or FARMING.)?

EXPAND: Does farming include (HUNTING or GROWING.) food?

STATE: The Vikings let their animals stay indoors in the <u>Winter</u>.

ASK: What season did the animals get to stay inside? (WINTER. or SUMMER)?

EXPAND: Would you say Winter is (COLD. or WARM)?
"Yes, Winter is cold!"
EXPAND: Do you like Winter? (LIKE or DISLIKE)?
Comment on the student's response.

STATE: The Vikings even had to clean up the animals' <u>poop</u>!

ASK: What did the Vikings clean up? Animal (POOP. or TOYS)?

EXPAND: And would you say that sounds (FUN or SICK!.)?

STATE: Let's say that a cow pooped 9 times in one day and then 4 times the next day. How many times did the cow poop?

ASK: So, what animal is pooping? (HORSE or COW.)?

EXPAND: How many times did it poop? (11 or 13.)?

STATE: Their writing system is called Runes. They wrote in different things like stone and jewels.

ASK: What did they write in stones and jewels? (RUNES. or BRAILLE)?

EXPAND: Do you think it would be (EASY or HARD) to carve characters into jewels or stone?
Comment on the student's choice.

STATE: They allowed people to vote.

ASK: What did their people get to do? (STEAL or VOTE.)?

EXPAND: Do you think voting sounds fun? (YES or NO)?
Comment on student response.

EXTENSION ACTIVITY: Have the student complete or write their own story problems about Vikings.

LESSON 4: ROSES

> **Main Cognitive Objective(s):** Students will acquire knowledge and gain understanding of roses.
>
> **Application of Math:** Began with math leading into the lesson.
>
> **Materials:**

STATE: Ok, let's figure out <u>even</u> and <u>odd</u> numbers.

ASK: We are figuring out even or (OLD or ODD.) numbers?

SPELL: Spell EVEN.

STATE: Even numbers end with <u>0,2,4,6</u> or <u>8</u>. (*Point to them on the letterboard or stencil to help them see the pattern of even and odd*)

ASK: So, 0,2,4,6,8 are (EVEN. or ODD) numbers?

EXPAND: Would 6 be an (EVEN. or ODD) numbers?

EXPAND: Would 9 be even? (YES or NO.)?

EXPAND: Is 18 an even number? (YES. or NO)?

STATE: Odd numbers end with <u>1,3,5,7</u> or <u>9.</u>

ASK: So, odd numbers end with 1,3,5, __ or 9? Is it (6 or 7.) the missing odd number?

EXPAND: Would 19 be (EVEN or ODD.)?

EXPAND: Is 7 an odd number? (YES. or NO)?

STATE: Now, let's say I have <u>25 roses</u>.

ASK: I have 25? (ANIMALS or ROSES.)?

EXPAND: And 25 is an (ODD. or EVEN) number?

EXPAND: Then let's say 5 were wilted. So how many are not wilted? (22 or 20.)?
"Wilted flowers are old and dying flowers or ones that don't have enough water."
EXPAND: And 20 is an (ODD or EVEN.) number?
"Yes that would be even."

STATE: Roses are a flower that come in all different <u>colors</u> and sizes.

ASK: So, a rose comes in different (NAMES or COLORS.)?

EXPAND: What is a common color of a rose? (BLUE or RED.)?

STATE: When people send another roses, sometimes they are sending a <u>messages</u> by the color of the rose.

ASK: So, when someone sends another roses, they could send a (MESSAGE. or SATIRE) through the color of the rose?

EXPAND: What do you think red could mean? Do you think it would mean (LOVE. or ANGER)?

STATE: A <u>dozen</u> roses is <u>12</u>.

ASK: if you get 12 roses than you have a (FEW or DOZEN.)?

EXPAND: And is 12 an (EVEN. or ODD) number?

STATE: <u>White</u> roses can mean <u>purity</u> or new beginnings.

ASK: What color means purity? (PINK or WHITE.)?

EXPAND: Would you say that pure is (CLEAN. or UGLY)?
"Yes, purity is an inner cleanliness if talking about a person."

STATE: Roses have <u>thorns</u> on the stems.

ASK: The stem of a rose has (THORNS. or THOUGHTS)?

EXPAND: Do you think that a thorn would be (SHARP. or DULL)?

STATE: Let's think about receiving <u>24</u> roses.

ASK: How many roses? (24. or 26)?

EXPAND: Is 24 an (EVEN. or ODD) number?
"Yes, because 24 ends in a 4."
EXPAND: If 12 is one dozen, then 24 would be (2. or 5) dozen?
"Yes, 24 is 12+12."

EXTENSION ACTIVITY: Have the student say if they enjoy roses. What is their favorite color of roses. How many roses did they think is the best amount to give someone.

LESSON 5: WHAT IS ART?

Main Cognitive Objective(s): Students will acquire knowledge and gain understanding of what is art.

Application of Math: Intersperse math into the lesson in connection to the topic.

Materials:

STATE: Throughout time, people have <u>debated</u> what is <u>art</u> and what is not art.

ASK: So, people have debated what is (ART. or COLOR)?

EXPAND: If you debate then you (AGREE or DISAGREE.)?
"Yep, when we debate we disagree with someone."
MATH: Let's say I debated <u>12</u> people on Sunday and <u>14</u> people on Tuesday. How many people did I debate? (30 or 26.)?
"That would be a lot of debates to have."
EXPAND: Now when you think of art, what do you think of? (DRAW. or SOCCER)? (PAINTING. or MAPPING)?

STATE: Art is a form of <u>expression</u>.

ASK: We would say, art is a form of (EXPRESSION. or FEAR)?

EXPAND: How else do we express ourselves? (READING or TALKING.)? (WRITING. or SITTING)?
"Those are good ways to express ourselves."
MATH: Let's say I expressed myself <u>67</u> times on Saturday, but only <u>42</u> of the times did someone listen. How many times was I not listened to? (25. or 26)?
"I think it is frustrating to be ignored!"

STATE: When we express ourselves in art, we are able to say things we can't say as well in everyday <u>words</u>.

ASK: In art, we express ourselves in (SPEECH or OTHER WAYS.)?

MATH: Let's say I expressed myself in art by drawing 15 paintings on Wednesday. But then my dog destroyed 4 of them. How many are still in good shape? (12 or 11.)?
"Let's hope it was one that wasn't too important!"
EXPAND: We can express ourselves in art through (MUSIC. or RUNNING)? (BEING STILL or DRAWINGS.)?

STATE: There are many different art forms. Some are music, dance, painting, poetry, and sculpting.

ASK: What is a form of art? (MUSIC. or MATH)?

EXPAND: What type of art do you prefer? (MUSIC or PAINTING)? (DANCING or POETRY)?

MATH: Let's say one day I did 44 spins in dance. On 22 of the spins I fell. How many was I able to stay standing in? (21. or 22)? And is that (MORE or LESS.) than half of the times I stayed standing?
"It takes practice to get good at things like this."

STATE: What you use to create a piece of art is called the medium. You might see by a work of art in a museum, "Medium: oil (paint) on canvas."

ASK: So, what is the thing we use to create a work of art? The (MEDIUM. or DEVICE)?

EXPAND: Would a medium possible be (CRAYONS. or FLOOR)?
"Crayons are a good medium to use."
MATH: Let's say I used the medium of oil 18 days in a row, two times each day. How many times did I use the medium of oil? (36. or 35) times?
"That is a lot of painting!"

STATE: We can draw with many different art media. As stated, the medium or (many—media) are the things we use like markers and crayons to draw or do something.

ASK: What things do we use to create drawings? (MARKERS. or CLAY)?

EXPAND: What else could we draw with? (PENCIL. or ERASER)? (ICE or PEN.)? (CHALK. or IRON)?
"Those are all good ideas."
MATH: If I colored with 45 crayons and broke 12 as I colored, how many aren't broken? (33. or 34)?
"It can be annoying to have a crayon break."

STATE: To create a painting, we can use a variety of paints or art media such as water colors, oils, and pastels.

ASK: Let's name a medium for painting? (PENS or WATER COLORS.)?

EXPAND: Watercolors are (FUN or BORING) to use?

MATH: If I have 10 water colors and I use 4 of them. How many are left unused? (5 or 6.)?
"Yes, one more over half."

STATE: To sculpt, one needs art media such as <u>clay</u>, hard <u>stone</u>, or even <u>soap</u>. Sculptors have to <u>carve</u> into or <u>mold</u> their words of art. They are <u>3D</u>.

ASK: What could be something we sculpt with? (FLOUR or SOAP.)?

SPELL: Let's spell CARVE and MOLD.

EXPAND: 3D means it is something with <u>depth</u>. Would a (CAR. or FLAT PICTURE) be 3D)?
"Yep, a car is 3D."
MATH: Let's think of some geometric 3D shapes. Would you say (SQUARE or CUBE.)? And (SPHERE. or CIRCLE)?
"Yes, cubes and spheres are 3D."

STATE: Art is an act of <u>expression</u> and <u>creativity</u>.

ASK: So, art is an act of (RETIREMENT or CREATIVITY.)?

EXPAND: Do you think sitting on the couch is a form of art (YES or NO.)?
"Most would probably say no to that one."
EXPAND: Is drawing a landscape a form of art? (YES. or NO)?

MATH: If I am creative 2 times a day for 10 days, how many times am I creative? (15 or 20.)?
"Yes, that would be 10 times."

EXTENSION ACTIVITY: *Student should write what their favorite kind of art to either do or look at is and why. If a student is not able to generate his or her own words, have him/her pick from choices to compose their short essay.*

...TILAGE

> **...e Objective(s):** Students will acquire knowledge and gain understanding of
>
> **Application of Math:** Intersperse math into the lesson in connection to the topic.
>
> **Materials:** picture of a skull, picture of baby head bound to make it longer

STATE: <u>Cartilage</u> is a white and <u>flexible</u> tissue in the body.

ASK: So, we are talking about (CARTILAGE. or BEEHIVES)?

SPELL: Spell FLEXIBLE.

EXPAND: Something flexible is (RAIN or <u>PLASTIC</u>.)?
"Yes, plastic or elastic are both flexible."

STATE: Cartilage can be found in your <u>ears</u>, (*help the student feel their ear to notice*) tip of your <u>nose</u>, (*show the picture of the skull to show how the tip of the nose is gone*) articulating <u>joints</u>, etc.
SKULL

ASK: Where do we find cartilage? (EARS. or EYES)? And also, your (JOINTS. or FLATBEDS)?

EXPAND: What word do you find in 'joints'? (<u>JOIN</u>. or ON)?
"Yes, your joints, so notice how the joints are where parts of the body join and bend."
EXPAND: I am going to touch with the back of my pencil a part of the body and you tell me if it is a joint. (*point to a spot and ask if it is a joint yes or no. Do this a few times.*)
YES OR NO

MATH: Let's say you have 14 joints in each hand. How many joints is that? (22 or <u>28</u>.)?
"Yes 14 plus 14 is 28." $14 + 14 = 28$

MATH: And if we don't count the 2 joints in each thumb how many total joints are there? (<u>24</u>. or 26)?
"Yes, because 2+2 is 4 so 28-4=24."

STATE: <u>Babies</u> are born with <u>300 bones</u> and lots of cartilage! Adults have <u>206</u> bones.

ASK: How many bones does a baby have? (<u>300</u>. or 200) bones?

MATH: How many more bones does a baby have than an adult? (80 or <u>94</u>.)?

SPELL: Spell BONES or CARTILAGE.

STATE: All the cartilage supports the rapid growth of the baby. Bones don't allow quick growth.

ASK: So, cartilage supports (SLOW or RAPID.) growth of a baby and child?
"Babies grow in so many ways quickly. Good thing it slows down as we age or else we'd be enormous."
EXPAND: Would you ~~said~~ SAY rapid goes with (FLIGHT or SPEED.)?

STATE: With time, cartilage is replaced with bone. Bones are fused together.

ASK: What is cartilage replaced with? (BONE. or HEIGHT)?

EXPAND: Do you think your longest bone is in your (LEG. or HEAD)?
"Yes, your leg. Your femur is quite long."
MATH: Let's say you broke your femur 3 times per year over 5 years. How many times did you break your femur? (15. or 16)? $5 \times 3 = 15$ $15 \times 2 = 30$

MATH: If 15 bones fused with 15 other bones, how many bones fused? (25 or 30.)?   BODY PART HAS 15 BONES. TWO OF THAT BODY PART = ? BONES

STATE: Since the heads of babies are flexible with cartilage, they are able to push through the birth canal. If they had been pure bone, that wouldn't work.
                                                              SOMETHING
ASK: The flexible cartilage in babies allows them to push through the (WATER or BIRTH.) canal?

EXPAND: Do you think the ability of the babies head to be flexible is (COOL or BORING)?

EXPAND: Some cultures they bind the babies head to make it longer (*show picture of baby with their head bound*). Could they do that if the babies head was made of pure bone? (YES or NO.)?

MATH: Let's say in 10 villages 4 baby's heads were bound each. How many baby heads would be bound? (40. or 104)?

MATH: And let's do 4x3? (12. or 14)?

STATE: Cartilage is important for our growth and for the structure and movement of our bodies.

ASK: Cartilage is important for (GROWTH. or SEASONS)?

SPELL: Spell STRUCTURE.

EXPAND: If your ears didn't have any cartilage, they would (HOLD UP Or FLOP.)?

EXPAND: Do you think you'd look good without cartilage? (YES or NO)?

MATH: Let's say there are 30 ears that have no cartilage and 15 people claim them. How many ears do the 15 people each get? (3 or 2.)?
"Yes, 30 divided by 15 is 2 since half of 30 is 15."

EXTENSION ACTIVITY: How the student write a story (with choices or with spelling) about a boy or girl without any cartilage.

SPELL   BODY   PART   BEGINNING   WITH   'N'
  "   "   "   "   "   'B'

  Λ   "   "   "   "   'H'

LESSON 7: ABRAHAM LINCOLN

Main Cognitive Objective(s): Students will acquire knowledge and gain understanding of Abraham Lincoln

Application of Math: Begin the lesson with math that leads into the lesson.

Materials:

STATE: A <u>foot</u> is <u>12 inches</u> long. A <u>yard</u> is <u>3</u> feet long.

ASK: So, a foot is (10 or 12.) inches long?

EXPAND: If a yard is 3 feet long than it is (34 or 36.) inches long?

EXPAND: Did you (MULTIPLE or ADD) to get that answer?
"Yes, you can do it either way."
EXPAND: If you wanted to give a speech to a large crowd, would you want to stand on a podium (3. or 1) feet high so everyone could see you?
"Probably a taller one so others could see you."

STATE: There was a man who became the <u>16th president </u>of the United States. He lived before there were <u>microphones.</u>

ASK: The 16th president of the United States did not have a (MIRCOPHONE. or JACKET)?

EXPAND: So, then if he wanted to speak with a large crowd and be seen and hear, he'd need to stand on a podium (2 FEET or 4 FEET.) high would be best?

MATH: If he stood on a podium 5 feet high and someone added 12 more feet to it, how high up would he be? (17. or 19) feet high?

MATH: And how many total yards could get from 17 feet? (5 YARDS. or 6 YARDS)?
"Yes, 3x5=15, plus 2 extra feet."

STATE: When Abraham was president there was <u>no television</u> or broadcasting services like <u>radio.</u>

ASK: When Lincoln was president there was no (TELEVISION. or CART AND HORSE)?

EXPAND: If you had no television or radio, do you think it would be (NORMAL or DIFFICULT)?
Comment on the student's response.

MATH: Let's say Lincoln went to the future and bought <u>25</u> big screen TVs one year and the next year he bought <u>32</u>. How many would he have altogether? (84 or 87.)?
"That would be crazy to have that many TV's don't you think!"

STATE: Abraham Lincoln grew up on a <u>farm</u> in <u>Illinois</u>. His mom died when he was young.

ASK: Who passed away when he was young? (DAD or MOM.)?

SPELL: Let's spell ILLINOIS since that is the state he grew up in.

MATH: Let's say on his farm he had 325 ears of corn and 414 blades of grass. How much altogether? (739. or 837)?

STATE: He called his step Mom his "<u>Angel Mother</u>" as she took good care of him and loved him.

ASK: What did he call his step mom? (ANGRY or ANGEL.) mother?

EXPAND: Would you call your mother your angel mother? (YES or NO)?
Comment about mothers.
MATH: If you mom gave you 39 pieces of candy one day and you ate 14. How much do you have left? (24 or 25.)?

STATE: He became a <u>lawyer</u> and ran for different government positions. Sometimes he <u>lost</u>.

ASK: Did Lincoln win all the elections? (YES or NO)?

EXPAND: What does this teach us? Would you say it tells you (NEVER GIVE UP. or DON'T TRY) it is too much work?

MATH: Let's pretend Lincoln ran for office 8 times and won 3 times. What is the ratio for how many times he won. Do you think it is (8/3 or 3/8.)?
"Yes, a ratio is a comparison."

STATE: He won the election in <u>1861</u> to become the 16th president of the <u>United States</u> of America.

ASK: Lincoln was the 16th president in the (NORTH KOREA or UNITED STATES.)?

MATH: If he was the 16th president, how many presidents came before him? (15. or 16)?

MATH: If Donald Trump is the 45th president. How many presidents between Lincoln to Trump? (27 or 29.)?

STATE: The <u>Southern</u> states in the USA were upset with the Northern states and wanted to <u>leave</u> the Union. While it wasn't directly about <u>slavery</u>, everything back then was about slavery.

ASK: Who was upset? (SOUTHERN. or NORTHERN) states?

EXPAND: Would slavery connected to (FREEDOM or OWNED.)?
"Yes, in slavery, someone owns you. They can treat you poorly or well. You are not paid money or are, but very little."
MATH: There were 33 states when Lincoln was president and 16 were southern states. How many were free Northern states with no slavery? (17. or 18)?
"Slaves, back then would try to escape to the norther states to be free."

STATE: As a result of the Southern states displeasure, the <u>Civil War</u> began. Lincoln fought to save the Union.

ASK: Lincoln wanted to (SAVE. or FORGET) the Union?

EXPAND: To save the Union he would want to (UNITE. or CONTROL) it?
"Yes, he thought the country should stay the United States of America."
MATH: Let's say 9 out of 16 southern states decided to join the Union again. How many would still be against the Union? (8 or 7.)?

SPELL: Spell CIVIL as a civil war is one that happens within a country.

STATE: In the end the Union was saved and the slaves were <u>freed</u>, but some hated Lincoln. He was <u>assassinated</u> by John Wilkes Booth.

ASK: The Union was saved and the slaves were (FREED. or SCARED)?

EXPAND: Assassinated would mean (KILLED. or ASSISTED)?

MATH: Let's say John Wilkes Booths had 29 guns and 17 were destroyed. How many does he have left? (12. or 11)?

EXTENSION ACTIVITY: Abraham Lincoln was sometimes referred to as the greatest USA president. Do you agree or disagree with this? What would make him great. Student should write about this or answer questions using choices to compose a reason.

LESSON 8: THE WILD BOAR AND FOX

Main Cognitive Objective(s): Students will acquire knowledge and gain understanding of the fable: "The Wild Boar and Fox

Application of Math: Random math facts throughout the lesson

Materials: pictures of a wild boar and of a fox.

STATE: One day a <u>wild boar</u> was sharpening his <u>tusk</u> (*present a picture of the wild boar with his tusk showing*) on a tree when along came a fox. (*present a picture of the fox*)

ASK: What was the wild board sharpening? (KNIFE or TUSK.)?

SPELL: And spell FOX.

EXPAND: Do you think the wild boar looks scary? (YES or NO0?
Comment on student response.
MATH: 29+9= (38. or 39)? And 30-12= (18. or 17)? (*Continue with more math problems if the student needs more regulation*)

STATE: Fox liked <u>teasing</u> him. So, he decided that he would ask all <u>scared</u> of the wild boar's sharp tusk.

ASK: The fox teased him by acting (MEAN or SCARED.)?

EXPAND: Do you think fox is (FUNNY or UNKIND)?
Comment on student response.
MATH: 33+45+ (76 or 78.)? And 87-23= (66 or 64.)? (*Continue with more math problems if the student needs more regulation*)

STATE: Boar just <u>kept</u> on working.

ASK: So, what did boar do? He just kept on (PLAYING or WORKING.)?

EXPAND: We could say that the wild boar (LIKE HIM or IGNORED.) him?
Comment on student response.
EXPAND: What do you think you'd do in this situation? (SMILE or BE MAD)?
Comment on student response.
EXPAND: Do you think the boar was (WISE or UNWISE) to ignore him?

Comment on student response.
MATH: 89-16= (72 or 73.)? And 7x8= (54 or 56.)?

STATE: At length, Fox asked Boar <u>why</u> in the world was he sharpening his tusk when there was <u>no danger</u> present!

ASK: Boar asked Fox (HOW or WHY.) he was sharpening his tusk when no danger was present?

EXPAND: What goes with danger? (POISON. or POPULATION)?
"Yes, anything that could harm you would be dangerous."
EXPAND: If you try to be safe are you a coward? (YES or NO.)?
"It is wise and sometimes brave to be safe."
MATH: If I have <u>10</u> wild boars and then <u>26</u> join me. Then <u>15</u> run away. How many do I have? (20 or 21.)?
Then if Mary runs 35 laps around wild boars, then 19 more. How many will she run altogether? (54. or 59)?

STATE: Boar answered, "true enough, but there is <u>no time</u> to get weapons ready when danger comes."

ASK: Boar things that there is (MORE TIME or NO TIME.) to get prepared when danger comes?

EXPAND: Do you think you should prepare (BEFORE. or WHEN) danger comes?
Comment on student's response.
MATH: 45/5= (10 or 9.)? And 18/3= (5 or 6.)?

EXPAND: What kind of danger might boar face that would require sharp tusk? (ANIMAL TRY TO EAT HIM. or FRIENDS LEAVE HIM)?
Comment on student's response.
EXPAND: What kind of danger might you face? Do you think it is more (PHYSICAL or EMOTIONAL) danger?
Comment on student's response.

STATE: All fables have a <u>moral</u> to them.

ASK: Fables have a (NAME Or MORAL.) to them did we say?

EXPAND: Moral goes with (VIRTUE. or MOTOR)?
"Yes, a moral is something we learn that is good to do."
MATH: 6x4= (23 or 24.)? And 3x7= (21. or 23)? Then 2x9= (16 or 18.)?

STATE: The moral of this story is to <u>prepare</u> beforehand to have a better guarantee of <u>safety</u> and <u>peace</u>.

ASK: If we prepare, then we will likely be more (SAFE. or AFRAID)?

EXPAND: Peace and safety could happen because the enemy would be (SCARED TO COME. or GLAD TO COME) since you are prepared?

MATH: 3x8= (22 or 24.)? And 5x6= (30. or 35)? Then 8x3= (22 or 24.)?

EXTENSION ACTIVITY: Have student write using choices or open ended how they prepare for danger. They should define what things could be a danger and how to prepare for those specific dangers. For those using choices you will ask questions to tease out the different answers and have them compose their thoughts.

LESSON 9: COLOR—FACTS AND TERMS

Main Cognitive Objective(s): Students will acquire knowledge and gain understanding of Facts and terms about colors.

Application of Math: Math facts throughout the lesson.

Materials: Box of crayons or markers with all the different hues. Have a 6 color, color-wheel picture available to show.

STATE: Today we will discuss <u>facts</u> and <u>terms</u> to know about colors in art.

ASK: So, we will be discussing different (FACTS or ACTIONS) connected to color?

SPELL: Let's have you spell TERMS.

EXPAND: Terms are (COMBINATIONS or WORDS.)?
"Yes, they'd be words we use."
MATH: Let's said we defined <u>52</u> terms and forgot <u>19</u> of them. How many terms did we remember? (34 or 33.)?
"Yes, learning 52 terms is a lot of effort! I would probably forget some of them."

STATE: Another name for <u>color</u> is the <u>hue</u>.

ASK: Ok, so I would like to know another name for color and that is? (HUE. or SHADOW)?

EXPAND: Now, let's see you know your colors. Let's see if you can tell me the hue.
(*Color with blue, then hold it up for the student to see*) What is the hue? (BLUE. or RED)?
(*Repeat with 2 to 9 more colors depending on student tolerance and enjoyment*)

MATH: Let's say you have 3 boxes with 8 hues in each. How many total hues? (23 or 24.)?

STATE: Now something more about colors. <u>Warm</u> colors are <u>red, yellow</u> and <u>orange</u>. (*Color on the page a smug of red, yellow and orange*) They have <u>longer</u> wavelengths.

ASK: The warm colors have (SHORTER or LONGER.) wavelengths?

ASK: Could you name the warm colors? (RED. or WHITE)? (GRAY or ORANGE.)? and (PURPLE or YELLOW.)?
"Yes, red, orange, and yellow. They are often bright!"
EXPAND: Warm colors might make you feel more (JOY. or SORROW)? (CALM or ANXIETY.)?

Comment on student response.
EXPAND: And you think...I think warm colors are (GOOD LOOKING or AWFUL)?
Comment on student response.
MATH: Let's say you had 36 warm colors and 6 boxes. How many warm colors would be in each box if you divided them evenly? (6. or 7)?

STATE: <u>Cool</u> colors are <u>blue</u>, <u>violet</u>, and <u>green</u>. They have <u>shorter</u> wavelengths.

ASK: Let's see, blue, violet and green would be (COOL. or WET) colors?

EXPAND: Now, I would like to know if cool color means cool as in, he's a (COOL DUDE. or NOT BRIGHT.)?
"Yes, they are not bright. They might be called dull."
MATH: Let's say my brother is a cool dude with 6 hats. He colors 7 different colors on each of them. How many colors altogether? (42. or 45)?

ASK: And literal, the cool colors have a (SHORTER. or LONGER) wavelength?

EXPAND: Would you see people wearing cool colors in the (WINTER. or SUMMER) usually?
"Often in the winter because they soak in the heat."

STATE: The <u>intensity</u> of a color is how <u>bright/ vibrant</u> or <u>dull</u> a color is.

ASK: So, we are talking about the (INTENSITY. or LIGHT) of a color?

EXPAND: Do you think (GRAY or RED.) will have more intensity?
"I'd say usually red is more intense because it is so bright. It is a challenge for gray to be intense."
MATH: Let's say I have 24 intense colors on my drawing and 15 dull colors. What is the difference in the amount? (8 or 9.)?
"Yes, as 24-15 is 9."
EXPAND: If some sports game is intense, then it will be (BORING or INTERESTING.)?
"Yes, intense sports games are usually interesting."
EXPAND: A game might be intense because the score is (CLOSE. or FAR) apart?
"Yes, if a game is intense, you will be saying, "I hope my team wins! Oh, dear! Come on! Come on! Let's go team!!"

STATE: <u>Contrast</u> is the <u>comparison</u> between colors. <u>High</u> contrast could be like a warm color next to a cool color. (*display color wheel for some of the questions below*)

ASK: So, contrast is a (SIGN or COMPARISON.) between colors?

EXPAND: Low contrast could be (BLUE/PURPLE. or RED/GREEN)?
"Yes, blue and purples are similar as purple has blue in it. So, they are low contrast."
EXPAND: High contrast could be (BLUE/GREEN or YELLOW/BLUE.)?
"Yes, because they are the opposite."
MATH: Let's say I have 19 pairs of high contrast colors. How many colors do I have? (39 or 38.)?
"19 plus 19 is 38."

STATE: Complementary are colors opposite on the color wheel. So, red & green, blue & orange, and yellow & purple. (*Show the color-wheel. Have the student point to the opposite colors as you talk.*) These are also the colors to make different brown if mixed.

ASK: So, colors opposite on the color wheel are (COMPLEMENTARY. or FORGETFUL) colors?
"Yep, they'd be complementary colors."
EXPAND: The complementary colors could be red and (GREEN. or ORANGE)? (*You can ask for the other combinations too. Again, eliminate choices when not needed throughout these lessons.*)

MATH: Let's say I had 3 groups with 4 red in each and 9 groups with 2 green in each. How many altogether? 4x3+ (11 or 12.)? And 9x2= (18. or 19)? Then 12+18= (29 or 30.)?
"We had to multiply and add to get the answer."

EXTENSION ACTIVITY/MOTOR ACTIVITY: *Student should create own color-wheel. Teacher should draw a circle and make 6 sections. Student should color each section the color it needs to be in order to be accurate. If it helps, clockwise colors are: red, orange, yellow, green, blue, purple. Rules for position of the clipboard, motor modeling, and independence apply here. Those really struggling with the motor or sensory tolerance should accept tries as good enough even if it means one mark on each of the 6 sections of the color wheel.*

LESSON 10: THE EYE

Main Cognitive Objective(s): Students will acquire knowledge and gain understanding of the eye.

Application of Math: Sprinkle math throughout the lesson that is not always related.

Materials: drawing of the eye (or be prepared to draw parts of the eye) from the side view— should include the optic nerve. Get small hand held mirror

---

STATE: A color has to do with light. Each color gives off a different wavelength when light bounces off of it, so we see different colors.

ASK: So, color has to do with (JOY or LIGHT.)?

ASK: Light travels to our eyes in (MONEY or WAVES.)?
"Yes, we see in waves!"
EXPAND: What organ in our body do we see color with? Would you say (PUTUITARY GLAD or EYES.)?
"Yes, our eyes are pretty incredible organs."
MATH: And let's do a little math. 7+14= (21. or 24)? Then 15+15= (32 or 30.)?

STATE: For us to see color, light from an object goes through our cornea. The cornea is a transparent part on the front of the eye. (*Show the picture of the cornea or draw it.*)

ASK: Let's see, could you tell me the transparent part on the front of the eye? (PUPIL or CORNEA.)?

EXPAND: Do you think transparent means (SEE THROUGH. or DARK)?
"Yes, if something is transparent, you can see through it. If you are transparent with your dad that means you are honest and clear about something."
MATH: If I see through 3 transparent doors on Thursday, but none on Friday. How many transparent doors did I see through? (3. or 4)?
"Yes, because 3+0=3."

STATE: Then you have a hole called the pupil. (*Point out the pupil. Have the student point to it.*)

ASK: The pupil is a (HOLE. or CAGE) in your eye?

EXPAND: Do you think it is safe to have a hole, like the pupil, in your eye? (YES or NO)?

38

MATH: 8 circles with 4 dots in each is (24 or 32.) circles?
"Yes, 8x4 or 8+8+8+8 is 32."

STATE: The colored part of your eye is the iris, which is a muscle that opens and closes your pupil letting more or less light in.

ASK: The iris is a (MUSCLE. or MEMORY)?

MATH: Let's see, 16 -13= (4 or 3.)?

EXPAND: Do you think your pupil will get (BIGGER or SMALLER.) if a room is very bright?
"Yes, they will get smaller so not as much light is let in."
EXPAND: Look at this mirror (*Show student their eye in the mirror*) What color is your iris? (*Give two choices if needed, one being the student's eye color*)

STATE: Behind the pupil is a lens. This helps focus the image of what you are seeing on the retina. (*Have the student point at the lens in the picture*)

ASK: The job of the lens is to (EXCLUDE or FOCUS.) an image on the retina.

EXPAND: If we focus, then we will see (WORSE or BETTER.)?

MATH: If a square has 4 sides and each side is 4 inches long. How many inches are all the sides (or the perimeter) altogether? (15 or 16.) inches?
"Yes, you could do 4x4 or 4+4+4+4 since a square by natures has sides of an equal length."

STATE: Your retina has photoreceptors called rods and cones. The cones help us to see the different colors and the rods light and dark. (*Have the student point to the retina.*)

ASK: We see color using our (CONES. or RODS)?

MATH: 10+40= (50. or 60)? And 40-10= (50 or 30.)?

EXPAND: A receptor will (RECEIVE. or REJECT) the image?
"Yes, receptors receive the images. If they don't do their job properly then it is hard to see."

STATE: The retina sends a message to the brain of what you are seeing through the optic nerve. (*Have the student point to the optic nerve*)

ASK: So, the retina sends a (JOKE or MESSAGE.) to the brain about what you are seeing?

EXPAND: When the message is sent through the optic nerve of the brain then you will (SEE. or SCREAM)?

"Yes, hopefully you see...once in a while you will scream if the image is scary."

MATH: Let's solve these problems. 5x8= (40. or 45)? And 35/7= (4 or 5.)?

EXTENSION ACTIVITY: *Have the student list as many parts of the eye as he or she can remember. Have the student pick an eye part to write about. Student should tell what it does and why it is important to see color.*

LESSON 11: VERBS AND MEASUREMENT

Main Cognitive Objective(s): Students will acquire knowledge and gain understanding of basic knowledge about verbs and the Mertic system verse US system of measuring.

Application of Math: Merge a math and English lesson.

Materials: ruler with centimeters and inches.

STATE: Did you know that <u>centimeters</u> are smaller than <u>inches</u>. (*display the ruler. Draw a cm and an inch.*)

ASK: Which is smaller? (CENITIMETER. or INCH)?

EXPAND: Now look, if I have 5 inches and 6 centimeters. (*trace 5 inches and 6 cm*) Which is longer? (INCHES. or CENTIMETERS)?
"Yes, even though there are more centimeters, the inches are much longer."

STATE: Let's say an ant <u>crawled 10</u> centimeters. (*draw 10 centimeters*)

ASK: What did the ant do? (CRAWL. or TALK)?

EXPAND: About how many inches is that? (*hold up the ruler with the inches next to the 10 centimeters for the student to see.*) Is it about (4. or 5) inches?
"Yes, just under 4 inches-3.94 inches."

STATE: Now, in we stated that the ant crawled 10 centimeters. The word crawled is a <u>verb.</u>

ASK: Crawled is a (VERB. or NOUN)?

EXPAND: Do you think that a verb would be a (THING or ACTION.)?

MATH: 10 centimeters is (GREATER THAN or LESS THAN.) 4 inches?
"Yes, it is just shy of 4 inches long at 3.94 inches."

STATE: Verbs are actions such as <u>jumped</u>, walked, and <u>sing</u>.

ASK: Verbs are (TIMES or ACTIONS.)?

EXPAND: Name a body part that is in action when we sing? (WRIST or MOUTH.)?
"Yes, also our voice box with the vocal cords…and even parts of the face have to move."

MATH: Let's say a ladybug jumped for 13 centimeters. (*trace 13 centimeters. Then lay the inches side of the ruler next to it for the student to see*) That is closer to (5. or 6) inches that the ladybug jumped?
"Yes, 5.12 inches."

STATE: Sentences can have <u>multiple</u> verbs in them. For example, <u>Pam bit an apple while running</u>.

ASK: Sentences can have (ONE or MULTIPLE.) verbs in them?

MATH: If Andy bit 2 inches (*trace 2 inches then lay the centimeter side next to it for the student to see*) into an apple, he would have bitten about how many centimeters? Close to (3. or 4) centimeters?
"Yes, that is 2.54 centimeters."
EXPAND: In that sentence the two verbs or actions words would be (BIT AND RUN. or PAM AND BIT)?
"Yes, because 'Pam' is a name and not an action."

STATE: Did you know that the <u>metric</u> system is a 10-based system. A <u>decameter</u> is 10 meters.

ASK: What is the metric system? A (10. or 15) based system?
"Our number system is too, just in the USA the measuring system is different."
EXPAND: Notice that the word decade is ten years. So 'deca' means (TEN. or TWELVE)?
"Yes, it is interesting."
EXPAND: 'Centi' means a <u>hundred</u> so think about century. How many years is a century? (100. or 200)?

STATE: Let's think about a sea turtle <u>swimming</u> for a <u>hundred</u> years (which some can by the way as they live a long time).

ASK: What is the verb that the sea turtle is doing? (HUNDRED or SWIMMING.)?

EXPAND: Do you think that is possible for one to swim non-stop for that long? (YES or NO.)?
"Probably can't do that non-stop. It would need some breaks but sea turtles can live a very long time."
MATH: Let's say a sea turtle was about a foot long. (*trace 12 inches and place the centimeters next to it*). How many centimeters is the sea turtle? About (29 or 30.) centimeters?
"Yep, it is 3.48 cm..."

STATE: In the sentence, '<u>Stanley doesn't articulate all his 'r' sounds,</u>' we should notice the verbs.

SPELL: Spell ARTICULATE.

EXPAND: The verb in this sentence is (ALL or ARTICULATE.)?
"Yes, the verb is articulate."

EXTENSION ACTIVITY: Measure different objects near the student. Find measurements in the metric system and US compared to the US system. Write a few more sentences and have the student identify the verbs.

LESSON 12: VOLUME OF A CUBE AND THE PRIMARY COLORS

Main Cognitive Objective(s): Students will acquire knowledge and gain understanding of the primary colors and measurements of volume

Application of Math: Begin with math and then mix it with the primary colors.

Materials:

STATE: If we want to measure the <u>space</u> in a bottle of paint we figure out the <u>volume</u>.

ASK: When we measure the space, we are measuring the (ENERGY or VOLUME.)?

EXPAND: And of course, space will be found (OUTSIDE or INSIDE.) the jar that we'd want to measure?
"Yes, we want to know how much space would be instead a container so we'd know how much we can fill it up with or say drink from?"

STATE: The volume of a cube is figured out by measuring <u>length x height x width</u>.

ASK: We do Length x Height x Width to figure out the volume of the (CUBE. or CYLINDER)?

EXPAND: And a cube will be the (SAME. or DIFFERENT) lengths on each side?
"Yes, because a cube is a 3D square."
EXPAND: So, if my cube has one side that is <u>5 inches</u>, the problem would be (5x5x5. or 5x5)?
(*can walk them through step by step if needed—like 5x5 is? Then 25x5 is?*) Then the volume would be (25 INCHES CUBED or 125 INCHES CUBED.)?

STATE: There are <u>three primary</u> colors.

ASK: How many primary colors? (THREE. or FIVE)?

SPELL: Spell PRIMARY.

STATE: The primary colors are the only colors that are <u>not made</u> my mixing other colors together.

ASK: The primary colors (ARE or AREN'T.) made by mixing other colors?

EXPAND: If you mix green and purple together will you get a primary color? (YES or NO.)?

"Right, this would not make a primary color but a tertiary color."
MATH: If you had a wanted to put a primary color in a cube that had the length of 3 inches. The problem would be (3x3 or 3x3x3.)? and the answer would be (27 INCHES CUBED. or 81 INCHES CUBED)?

STATE: The primary colors are the <u>foundation</u> colors that are <u>mixed</u> to make other colors.

ASK: So, primary colors are (ANNOYING or FOUNDATION.) colors?

EXPAND: Is a foundation at the (BOTTOM. or TOP) of a house?
"Yes, because a foundation is what you build something on. For homes, it is often concrete."
EXPAND: Without a foundation, a house would (FALL. or IGNITE)?
"Yes, it would fall down. It would not have support when trouble comes."
EXPAND: So, then, without the primary colors we'd have (ALL or NO.) other colors?

STATE: The primary colors are <u>red, yellow</u> and <u>blue</u>.

ASK: So, what are the primary colors? (RED. or GRAY)? (PINK or BLUE.)? and (YELLOW. or CHOCOLATE)?
"Yes, and those primary colors make other colors."
MATH: How many inches cubed would I have for blue paint in a cube shaped container that is 8 inches long? First, the problem would be (8x8x8. or 8x8)? And 8x8= (63 or 64.)? Now 64x8. 8x4= (32. or 33)? We carry over the 3 so 8x6+3= (50 or 51.)? So, the answer is (512. or 51) inches cubed?

EXPAND: OK, let's think of some things that are red. (*Have student list two or three red things. Give choices if needed. Same for the following two*) (DOOR or CARDINAL BIRD.)?
"It could also include a stop sign. Of course, the octagon shape with red triggers the symbol to stop even without the words 'stop' on it."
EXPAND: Alright, now let's list some things that are yellow. (RUBBER DUCK. or TV SCREEN)? (SCHOOL BUS. or PLUM)
"Yes, now they are making rubber ducks other colors than yellow."
EXPAND: Now, last let's list things that are blue. Would you say (FAUCET or SKY.)? and (BLUEBERRIES. or CARROTS)?
"Yes, but blueberries are not a pure blue. They almost look purple when you break them open and get the juice on yourself."

STATE: Let's think about another <u>cube</u> that is 10 inches long.

SPELL: Let's spell CUBE just for fun!

EXPAND: To calculate, let's do 10x10 which equals? (100. or 110)?

"Yes, so anything times ten is the number plus the zeros. So 1x1= 1 and then 2 zeros so you know the answer is 100."

EXPAND: And then 100x10. Remember 1x1 then add the zeros. So, then the volume is (1,100 or 1,000) inches cubed.

EXTENSION ACTIVITY: Have the student pick the favorite primary color and give reasons why it is the best color...use choices if needed.

LESSON 13: VOLCANOES

Main Cognitive Objective(s): Students will acquire knowledge and gain understanding of volcanoes

Application of Math: Math mixed into the lesson topic

Materials: picture of layers of the earth and a picture of a volcano.

STATE: Under the thin layer of the earth's <u>crust</u>, which we live on, lies the <u>mantle</u> which is quite a bit thicker than the crust. (*present picture of the layers of the earth*)

ASK: Under the earth's crust lies the (MANTLE. or TROPOSPHERE)?

EXPAND: Let's say the earth was 150 feet thick and the mantle is 1,345 feet thick. How many feet thick total? (1,495 FEET. or 1,395) feet thick?
"Yes, that would actually be quite thin."

STATE: The mantle's temperature can become <u>7,230</u> degrees <u>Fahrenheit</u> (4,000 degree Celsius). As you can imagine you wouldn't live if you touched the mantle.

ASK: How many degrees Fahrenheit? (4,000 or 7,230.)?

MATH: The coolest levels of the mantle are about 392 degrees Fahrenheit. What is the difference between the warmest and coolest temperatures in the mantle? 7,230-392= (7,838, or 6,838.)? (*walk them through the subtraction process if needed.*)

EXPAND: Why do you think you wouldn't live if you touched the mantle? (BURN UP. or MAGICAL DISAPPEARANCE)?
"Yes, depending on the humidity human's cells start to die around 106 degrees Fahrenheit. In dry air with water and some access to cooler temperatures you could live for a while in temperatures of 150 degrees Fahrenheit."

STATE: The mantle is made up of <u>silicate</u> minerals which are <u>rock</u> forming minerals.

ASK: So, what kind of minerals is the mantle made up of? (SILICATE or DELICATE) minerals?

EXPAND: We can assume that the mantle helps form (SEA GRASS or ROCK.)?
"Yes, rock doesn't melt, it morphs and changes to different types of rocks. There is even a rock cycle."
MATH: If the mantle formed 3,000 rocks and then 400 were destroyed. How many rocks would be left? (2,600. or 3,400)?

STATE: The mantle has <u>magma</u> in the upper part. When the magma reaches the surface of the earth and starts to come, we now have a <u>volcano</u>.

ASK: When magma comes to the crust we have an (EARTHQUAKE or VOLCANO.)?

EXPAND: So, then can we have a volcano inside the mantle? (YES or NO.)?

EXPAND: Do you think (PRESSURE. or WIND) is involved in the formation of a volcano?
"Yes, pressure would need to push it up. Has to do with thermal expansion."
MATH: If you put pressure on your arm for 27 minutes and then for 43 minutes more. Would this be (OVER. or UNDER) an hour of putting pressure on your arm?

STATE: Volcanoes act in different ways. Some explode and are called <u>Composite</u> or strato-volcanoes.

ASK: Volcanoes with huge eruptions are called (COMPOSITE. or DEPOSITED) volcanoes?
"Mount St Helens in Washington USA is a composite volcano."
EXPAND: Do you think it would be more interesting to watch a(n) (EXPLOSIVE or CALM) volcano?
Comment on the student's response.
MATH: Let's say one volcano exploded 90 feet in the air and another 24 feet in the air. How many feet altogether? (104 or 114.) feet?

STATE: When magma reaches the surface, it is now called <u>lava</u>. <u>Shield</u> volcanoes rarely explode but have rapid moving lava.

ASK: Which volcano has rapid moving lava? (COMPOSITE or SHIELD.)?

EXPAND: Which seems more dangerous? (SHIELD or COMPOSITE) volcanoes?
"Composite volcanoes are more deadly. Shield volcanoes, like Hawaii, are rarely deadly even though they erupt a lot. The sides of these volcanoes are NOT steep."
MATH: If lava from a shield volcano traveled 60 mph for 3 hours. How far will it have traveled? (180 MPH. or 360 MPH)?

STATE: The <u>dome</u> volcano has slow moving lava. The sides are <u>steep</u>, but it cools and hardens relatively quickly.

ASK: Now we are talking about a (SHIELD or DOME.) volcano?

EXPAND: Which seems more deadly to you? (SHIELD or DOME)?

Comment on student's response.

MATH: If the lava from a dome volcano was moving at 4 miles per hour for 3 hours. How many miles would it have traveled? (9 or 12.)?

EXTENSION ACTIVITY: Have the student write a summary of the three volcanoes. If they are not able to compose independently, give them choices to review the three volcanoes discussed.

LESSON 14: SYMBOLS OF NEUTRAL COLORS

Main Cognitive Objective(s): Students will acquire knowledge and gain understanding of symbols and feelings produce by the neutral colors.

Application of Math: Math mixed into the lesson topic.

Materials: brown, black, gray, and white color tools (like crayons)

STATE: <u>Neutral</u> colors include colors such as black, brown, white and gray. (*color with each crayon as you say it.*)

ASK: We are talking about (WHOLE or NEUTRAL.) colors?

MATH: Let's just do a few warm up problems for a second. 4x5= (20. or 25)? And 6x3= (17 or 18.)?

EXPAND: If your friends are having an argument about who is the coolest and you are staying out of it, you could also say you are (MEAN or NEUTRAL.)
"Yeah, neutral means you don't take sides. Some people believe that neutral colors fit with all colors."

STATE: Let's talk about what neutral colors can <u>represent</u> when doing some art.

ASK: We are talking about how colors represent different things in (ART. or MUSIC)?

EXPAND: If I represent something or someone I (REGRET or STAND FOR.) that thing?
"Yes, the early American colonist, didn't feel they were represented in England so then there was a war."
MATH: If you used 18 different neutral colors on an assignment and then cut out half of them, how many would be left? (8 or 9.)?

STATE: Now <u>brown</u>, can help us feel <u>comfortable</u> or like at home. It also can represent <u>earth</u>.

ASK: So, brown can create a feeling of (COMFORT. or FREEDOM)?

MATH: If 26 out of 78 numbers felt uncomfortable, how many were comfortable? (51 or 52.)?

EXPAND: Earth makes us think of (SOIL. or MONEY)?
"I usually think of soil when I think of earth."
EXPAND: I think the color brown is (UGLY or PRETTY)?

50

STATE: <u>Black</u> can represent <u>night</u> or <u>evil</u>.

ASK: Night can be represented with the color (RED or BLACK.)?

EXPAND: If you want to show someone is not to be trusted in a picture, but wants to do bad things you could paint them with (WHITE or BLACK.)?
Comment on student response.
EXPAND: Do you think that night goes best with (DARKNESS. or DELIGHT)?

MATH: Let's say I drew 18 people in black on one page and 25 people in black on another page. How many people are drawn in black? (42 or 43.)?

MOTOR ACTIVITY: Let's just color accord this page a bunch of black for the night sky with big strokes (*Hold up the clip board with paper on it. Motor model if needed before letting student do it themselves. Remember, for those who really struggle, a try, even a line or two can count as good enough.*)

STATE: <u>White</u> often stands for <u>purity</u>, good and <u>reverence</u>.

ASK: So, goodness could be represented with the color (PINK or WHITE.)?

EXPAND: Who might you color white in a picture? Would it be a (ROBBER or ANGEL.)?

MATH: If I had a painting full of 5 angels, each hold 6 harps. How many harps would that be? (30. or 25)?

EXPAND: To be pure is to be (WEIRD or CLEAN.)?

STATE: Gray is a color that sometimes stands for <u>old age</u>, <u>boredom</u> or <u>security</u>.

ASK: Ok, the color gray can stand for (OLD. or YOUNG) age?

EXPAND: And, if you are old, will your (HAIR. or NOSE) turn gray?
"Yeah, the nose doesn't change much with age. But the hair is usually noticeable unless someone dyes it a lot."
EXPAND: Do you think of boredom when you see gray? (YEP or NOPE)?
Comment on student's response.
MATH: Let's say I was bored for 15 minutes of a 25-minute lesson. How many minutes was I interested in the lesson? (8 or 10.)?
Comment on student response.

EXPAND: Who would want to put gray on some art to show security? Could it be a (BANK. or FUN CENTER)?

"Yes, fun centers would need bright or fun colors. Banks are more serious places."

EXTENSION ACTIVITY: *List two more words for brown, white, black, and gray that those colors could represent. Give the student options if needed.*

LESSON 15: TENKAMENIN—KING OF GHANA

Main Cognitive Objective(s): Students will acquire knowledge and gain understanding of Tenkamenin, king of Ghana from 1037 AD/CE to 1075 AD/CE

Application of Math: Math mixed into the lesson

Materials: picture of Tenkamenin, map of Africa that shows Ghana

STATE: Tenkamenin, king of <u>Ghana</u>, reigned between <u>1037-1075</u> AD (CE).

ASK: We are talking about the king of (FRANCE or GHANA.)?

MATH: If he reigned from 1037 to 1075, how many years was he the king? (38. or 40) years? (*If needed, walk him through each step of the math problem.*)

EXPAND: While the boarders for Ghana have changed since then, what part of Africa is Ghana in? (*display a map of Africa*) (EAST or WEST.)?

STATE: Many believe that had it not been for <u>Tenkamenin</u> and his reign in Ghana, Ghana wouldn't have ever reached its <u>height</u> of greatness.

ASK: Tenkamenin, helped Africa reach its (CLOSURE or HEIGHT.) of greatness?

EXPAND: We could say, height of greatness could be renamed as its (PEAK. or SOLITUDE)?

MATH: Let's say Ruth did 29 great things and Ansh did 42 great things. How many more great things did Ansh do than Ruth? (12 or 13.)?

EXPAND: Do you think greatness would be (POWERFUL. or NATURAL)?
Comment on student's response.

STATE: King Tenkamenin is still known as the person who <u>facilitated</u> the <u>Saharan</u> Gold Trade.

ASK: What type of gold trade did Tenkamenin help facilitate? (RICHMAN'S or SAHARAN.) Gold Trade?
"Sahara is a desert in northern Africa."
EXPAND: Would you say facilitated is to (SACRIFICE or MAKE POSSIBLE.)?

MATH: 12 brothers facilitated the 12 missions each. How many missions were facilitated by the 12 brothers altogether? First, we should (DIVIDE or MULTIPLY.) to answer this question? And the answer is (144. to 134)?

STATE: Ghana was very <u>wealthy</u> and was often referred to as the "Land of <u>Gold</u>."

ASK: The people of Ghana were very (OLD FASHION or WEALTHY.)?

EXPAND: And you'd connect wealthy with the word (ABUNDANCE. or ATROCITY)?
"Wealthy people can have an abundance of things."
MATH: Musa own 43 gold nuggets. His enemy stole 14. How many gold nuggets does he have left? (29. or 28)?

EXPAND: When you think of gold, do you think of (POVERTY of CALIFORNIA)?
"Yes, California had a gold rush in the 1800's. Poverty could cause one to look for gold."

STATE: They controlled trade routes between <u>salt</u> and gold mines. If you wanted <u>protection</u>, they'd trade it for gold nuggets.

SPELL: Spell GOLD since they controlled trade routes for gold mines.

ASK: And they also controlled trade routes for (SAND or SALT.) mines?

EXPAND: Would you give them gold for protection? (YES or NO)?
Comment on student response with your opinion.
MATH: If you had a nugget of gold that was 5 cm long, one that was 6 cm long, another 2 cm long, and the last 4 cm long. How many centimeters long altogether? (17. or 18)?
"They believe the largest gold nugget ever found was 6.6 cm long."

STATE: Education in Ghana back then came mainly from storytellers they called <u>griots</u>.

ASK: What did they tell their storytellers? (GRIOTS. or ORATORS)?

EXPAND: Do you think education is best when it is presented in a (STORY or LIST OF FACTS)?
Comment on student's response.
MATH: Ryan took 35 minutes to tell his grandma about camp, 45 minutes to tell him mom about school, and 13 minutes to tell his baby sister a story. How long did Ryan take talking to everyone? (93 MINUTES. or 90 MINUTES)?

STATE: Since Tenkamenin <u>managed</u> the trade so carefully Ghana reached its height of greatness. His strength however was more in governance and not <u>economics</u>.

ASK: Tenkamenin's strength was in (GOVERNANCE. or ECONOMICS)?

"We'll find out why in just a bit."

EXPAND: To manage is to (INFLUENCE or GUIDE AND OVERSEE.) do you think?

MATH: If you managed 3 more bank accounts each hour for 4 hours strait, how many bank accounts would you be managing by the end of 4 hours? (11 or 12.)?

STATE: Daily, King Tenkamenin, went through his empire on horseback <u>listening</u> to everyones problems. He made sure justice had been served before he left their presence.

ASK: What did King Tenkamenin do for his people? (DESTROY or LISTEN.)?

EXPAND: Do you think people want to be (LISTENED TO or HEAR ALL A PERSON'S KNOWLEDGE) the most?

Comment on the student's response.

EXPAND: Have you ever hear the saying "No one cares what you know until they know you care." Do you (AGREE or DISAGREE) with this?

Comment on student's response.

MATH: Olga listened to Hector for 24 minutes, Jason for 13 minutes, Aparna for 27 minutes. How long did Olga listen to everyone altogether? (64. or 74) minutes?

EXTENSION ACTIVITY: Have students say if it is more important to make a country wealthy or compassionate/listening to each other. Then have the student say why or why not. Use choices if needed.

LESSON 16: SYMBOLIC MEANING OF PRIMARY COLORS

Main Cognitive Objective(s): Students will acquire knowledge and gain understanding of the symbolic meaning of primary colors.

Application of Math: Math mixed into the lesson topic

Materials: red, blue, and yellow coloring tools. (like crayons)

EXPAND: When you are really mad, do you think of (LAVANDER or RED) that goes best with angry?

"Many people think of the color red because people become red in the face when they are mad."

MATH: If Fred was mad 8 times Friday, 12 times Saturday, and 15 times Sunday. How many times was Fred mad in 3 days? (34 or 35.) times?

STATE: Artist use different <u>colors</u> in their paintings to <u>convey</u> feelings, <u>emotions</u>, get your <u>focus</u> on a part of the picture and a sometimes a story.

ASK: So, an artist could use color to convey (MUSCLES or EMOTIONS.)?

SPELL: How about spell COLOR since color is used to convey things such as emotion in art.

MATH: If I had 24 emotions on Wednesday and 13 on Thursday. How many emotions did I have altogether? (35 or 37.)?

"That is a lot of emotions! I wonder how many we have everyday!"

EXPAND: If you convey something, then you (COMMUNICATE. or HIDE)?

"Yes, you might convey a message to a friend, or if you start getting up in the air in a session, you convey to me that you need some math ☺ "

MATH: (*Turn to the math side of the letterboard or produce the number stencil and have the student write their own math problem and solve it. Do at least 2 and continue if student needs to do more to calm.*) I'd like to see you write and solve your own math problem. Let's do a few.

EXPAND: Let's name some emotions. How about (RUNNING or FEAR.)? and would you say (JOY. or DISAPEAR)?

STATE: <u>Red</u> is used to show <u>anger</u>. But red can also represent <u>love</u> or convey <u>power</u>.

ASK: So, red can convey (LOVE. or CALM)?

EXPAND: If you wanted to show someone was full of love with the color red, where would you color or paint red (LIPS or HEART)?

Comment on the student's choice.

MATH: Let's say Alexandra was full of love for 15 boys on Monday but by Friday she decided she only liked 4 of them. How many did she decide she doesn't love? (11. or 12)?

EXPAND: If you wanted to show someone was mad with red, would you put red on the (FACE. or HANDS)?

"Probably the face, since that is where we display our emotions. A clenched fist when someone is mad could easily be white."

EXPAND: If you wanted to show someone was powerful, would you put the red on their (FACE or CLOTHES)?

MATH: Martin flexed his muscles 6 times each hour for 7 hours. How many times did he flex his muscles? (42. or 49)?

"I wonder what kind of guy would do that ☺"

STATE: <u>Yellow</u> can be used to represent things such as <u>sunlight</u>, <u>happiness</u>, and <u>joy</u>.

ASK: So, a color that can represent joy is (YELLOW. or GREEN)?

MATH: Krassi inflated 12 smiley faced balloons for her friend's birthday party. But her friend popped 4 of them. How many are left? (7 or 8.)?

"I wonder if you would want to have smiley face balloons around? (YES or NO)?"

EXPAND: When you see a picture of bright yellow sunflowers would you feel (SICK or HAPPY) do you think?

Comment on student's response.

MATH: (*Turn to the math side of the letterboard or produce the number stencil and have the student write their own math problem and solve it. Do at least 2 and continue if student needs to do more to calm.*) Go ahead and write and solve your own math problem.

EXPAND: Do you think you might use the color yellow to convey happiness in a picture? (YES or NO)?

MATH: 14x2= (34 or 28.)? Then 24+7= (31. or 32)? And 14x4= (56. or 58)?

STATE: Now, let's think about <u>blue</u>. Blue can be for <u>depression/sadness</u>. It can also go with <u>calmness</u> and <u>peace</u>.

ASK: If I wanted to show someone that my character was sad in my painting, I might paint them (BLUE. or ORANGE)?

MATH: Bobby made 4 sad choices in the morning, 9 in the afternoon, and 24 in the evening? How many sad choices were made? (37. or 38)?

"I think Bobby needs to go to bed. Seems like tiredness set in by the evening!"

EXPAND: We could also help someone feel (ANNOYED or CALM.) if we paint with blue?

EXPAND: Do you prefer to feel (PEACE or HONOR)?

Comment on the student's response.

MATH: 35/7= (5. or 6)? And 3x6= (18. or 20)? Then 30x5= (120 or 150.)?

EXTENSION ACTIVITY: *Student should write a short story called "THE BLUE DAY." If student can't compose independently, then have student pick from choices to compose it.*

OR

Write a story problem using information from this lesson. Use choices if needed.

LESSON 17: CAMELS

Main Cognitive Objective(s): Students will acquire knowledge and gain understanding of camels

Application of Math: Math mixed into the lesson topic

Materials: picture of a camel, map of Africa.

STATE: A <u>camel</u> will not spit at you for fun. A camel will <u>spit</u> at you if it feels threatened.

ASK: We are talking about a (BEAR or CAMEL.)?

EXPAND: And if a camel spit at you, would you (SPIT BACK or RUN)?
Comment on student's response.
MATH: If <u>7 camels</u> spit at you <u>3</u> times, how many times would the camel have spit at you? (20 or 21.)?

STATE: Camels can drink <u>40 gallons</u> of water in one sitting and go without water for a longer time than you or I can, thus making them great for traveling with in a <u>desert</u>.

ASK: Camels can drink (30 or 40.) gallons of water in one sitting?

SPELL: Spell GALLON.

EXPAND: In the desert, would you sweat off water (FASTER. or SLOWER) than on a nice spring day?
"Yes, all the heat will cause you to sweat as your body tries to cool down."
MATH: If a camel drank <u>40</u> gallons of water <u>8</u> times in a row, how many gallons of water would that be? (320. or 480)?

STATE: A camel <u>stores fat</u>, not water in their <u>humps</u>. However, this fat can be changed into food or water if needed.

ASK: What does a camel store in his or her humps? (WATER or FAT.)?

EXPAND: If you had a hump somewhere on your body, would you prefer to store (SWEETS or WATER) in it?
Comment on student's response.
MATH: You see <u>35</u> camels with <u>2</u> humps each. How many humps is that? (65 or 70.)?

STATE: Did you know that the word 'camel' comes from an <u>Arabic</u> word that means '<u>beauty</u>.'

ASK: Camel comes from an (EUROPEAN or ARABIC.) word meaning beauty?
"Arabic is a cursive language. They do not use letters of the alphabet that we do in English or Spanish."
EXPAND: Do you think camels are beautiful (YEP or NOPE)?
Comment on the student's response.
MATH: If you met <u>435</u> camels that were beautiful and found <u>231</u> dead the next day, how many would you say are left? (204. or 304)?

STATE: Those <u>Arabian</u> camels have only one hump (*draw one hump*) while Asian camels have <u>2.</u> (*draw two humps*)

ASK: So, Arabian camels have (1. or 2) humps?

SPELL: Let's spell HUMP since it is a short word and we are talking about humps.

EXPAND: So, you think you would prefer to ride on an (ASIAN or ARABIAN) camel?
Comment on student's response.
MATH: Asma rode on her camel for <u>25 Kilometers</u>. She took a break. Then she rode on her camel for <u>34</u> more kilometers. How many kilometers did she ride altogether? (57 or 59.)?

STATE: The mouths of camels are <u>thick</u> and they can eat <u>thorny</u> plants that other animals can't eat because of it.

ASK: What part of the camel did we say is thick? (EYES or LIPS.)?

EXPAND: If something is thorny then it could (POKE. or TICKLE) you?
"Most likely poke you! If you brushed against a dull thorn, it might tickle you."
EXPAND: What do you think? Would it hurt more to sit on a (TACK or get poked by a THORN)?
Comment on student's response.
MATH: Kristin was poked by <u>15 thorns</u> on her walk through the field to her friends. Then she was poked <u>32</u> times on her way back. How many times was she poked? (47. or 49)?

EXPAND: Do you think it was wise for her to walk back through the field after having been poked so many times? (YES or NO)?
Comment on student's response.

STATE: In some <u>Middle Eastern</u> countries camels are considered a <u>delicacy</u>.

ASK: So, some Middle Eastern countries, camel is a (DELICACY. or FRENCH PASTRY)?

EXPAND: If something is a delicacy, will the (RICH. or POOR) eat it?
"Yes, delicacies are usually eaten by the rich."
EXPAND: Would you like to eat camel do you think? (YEP or NOPE)?
Comment on student's response.
MATH: Abdulah had <u>14</u> piece of camel on his plate. He ate <u>6</u> of them. How many did he have left? (7 or 8.)?

EXTENSION ACTIVITY: Have the student draw a desert scene. Motor model (hand over hand) each part and then have the student do it by themselves. Start simple and increase complexity with student according to student's tolerance level and success level.

LESSON 18: THERMAL EXPANSION

Main Cognitive Objective(s): Students will acquire knowledge and gain understanding of thermal expansion

Application of Math: Math intertwined in the lesson

Materials: picture of Eiffel Tower, picture of expansion joints like for a bridge

---

STATE: Two or more atoms make a <u>molecule</u>.

ASK: What are two or more atoms together? A (MOLECULE. or TWO-SUM)?

EXPAND: Think about a water molecule. Now would atoms be (TINY. or LARGE)?
"They are smaller than microscopic!"
MATH: Think of 20 atoms. Now thing of 40 atoms and 30 atoms. How many atoms is that? (100 or 90.)?

STATE: If molecules are moving at <u>20 miles </u>an hour for <u>3</u> hours. How many miles have they traveled?

ASK: How many miles are the molecules moving per hour? (15 or 20.)?

EXPAND: And how many miles will they have traveled in 3 hours. (60. or 70)?

STATE: Molecules that are <u>cold</u>, are <u>densely</u> packed together and move slowly.

ASK: If molecules are cold the they will be (DENSELY. or PRECISELY) packed together?

EXPAND: Think of yourself in a group outside in the cold. Would you stand (FAR AWAY or CLOSE TOGETHER.)?
"Most people would stand close together next to other people.
MATH: 37 freezing molecules huddled together, 42 joined them. How many molecules altogether? (79. or 80)?

STATE: Let's think of molecules moving at <u>59 miles</u> per hour. Now consider that they stayed at a constant rate for the <u>4 hours</u>. How many miles would they have traveled for.

ASK: We are thinking about molecules moving how fast? (52 or 59.) mph? And for how long? (4. or 5)?

"Yes, so let's think of what we do first. Look at the ones column.

EXPAND: We would say 4x9= (36. or 26)?

"We carry over and now what do we have!"

EXPAND: And we'd say 4x5+3= (23. or 24)?

EXPAND: And the final answer is? (235 or 236.) miles?

STATE: When molecules are <u>warm</u>, the move quickly and <u>expand</u> out thus making them less dense.

ASK: Warm molecules will be (MORE or LESS.) dense?

EXPAND: Which will weigh more if warm molecules are less dense than cold molecules? (COLD. or WARM)?

"Yes, because they are more densely packed together."

MATH: If 147 molecules are moving quickly and then 35 cool down. How many are still moving quickly and are warm? (112. or 123)?

EXPAND: Ok when you open a warm oven, the heat hits you in the (FEET or HEAD.)?

"Yes, the face because it is warm air and it rises as it weighs less than the air outside the oven."

STATE: Thermal has to do with <u>heat</u> and <u>temperature</u>. Think of <u>thermometer</u> and thermals.

ASK: Thermal has to do with (HEAT. or WATER)?

EXPAND: What word would you make up to mean 'my face is hot'? (THERMOFACE or THERMOSKINWARMER)?

Comment on student's response."

MATH: Lily was in a warm room for 5 hours on Monday. How many hours was she not warm on Monday? (18 or 19.)?

"Yes, because remember that a day has 24 hours in it."

STATE: Thermal expansion is most obvious with <u>gases</u> but it also happens to <u>solid</u>s.

ASK: Thermal expansion is most obvious with (SOLIDS or GASES.)?

EXPAND: Name a gas. (OXYGEN. or PLASTIC)?

MATH: Matthew, Soumil, and Cindi sat in gases for 34 minutes each. How many minutes did they sit in gases for? (102. or 103) minutes?

STATE: The _Eiffel_ Tower (*Show picture of Eiffel Tower*) increases <u>13 cm</u> in the Summer time compared to Winter.

ASK: When does the Eiffel Tower increase 13 cm? (WINTER or SUMMER.)?

EXPAND: This would be a result of (THERMAL. or DYNAMIC) expansion?

MATH: If the Eiffel Tower didn't contract back in the winter for 5 years and so increased 13 cm each year, how much taller would it be after 5 years? (65. or 70) cm taller?

STATE: Architects and engineers account for thermal expansion when they build things like <u>bridges</u>. They put expansion joints into the bridges. (*show expansion joints and show how they give room for them to contract and expand*)

ASK: What is an architectural structure that they account for thermal expansion? (BRIDGE. or SEABANK)?

SPELL: Spell EXPANSION JOINTS

MATH: If a bridge 300 feet long and has expansion joints every 20 feet. How many expansion joints are on the bridge? (14 or 15.)?

EXTENSION ACTIVITY: Have the student help you bake something. Have them feel the heat rise as you open the over to put the food in and take it out. Student can write out the experience. Use choices if needed to answer questions about the observations and experiences made.

LESSON 19: A DAY AT THE BEACH

Main Cognitive Objective(s): Students will acquire knowledge and gain understanding of a picture reading with a beach and facts about the beach or ocean.

Application of Math: Math intertwined in the lesson

Materials: picture of a beach...should show sand, ocean with waves, seashells, people...you can get a few different beach pictures for the lesson to show different types

STATE: Let's take a look at this <u>beach</u> (*present a picture of the beach and help the student look at it*).

ASK: We are looking at a (BEACH. or FARM)?

EXPAND: If we didn't already know, we can tell from the picture that beaches are by the (OCEAN. or COUNTRY FAIR)?

STATE: Some people like to <u>collect seashells</u> at the beach. Ronald and his sister Nina were no different. They collected <u>98</u> seashells are Friday and <u>76</u> on Saturday.

ASK: So, some people like to collect (MAIL or SEASHELLS.) did we say?

EXPAND: Let's think about how many they collected. So, 6+8 is (14. or 15)?
"And we carry the 1 over and put the 4 down below the ones column."
EXPAND: 7+9+1= (16 or 17.)?

EXPAND: So, then our answer would be? (174. or 175.)?

EXPAND: If you collected seashells, would you collect (LARGE or SMALL) seashells?
Comment student's response.

STATE: Now take a look at this picture again (*hold up the same one or indicate if you want them to look at a new one*) Look at the <u>waves</u> and see what you notice about them. (*draw attention to the waves*)

ASK: We are looking at the (WAVES. or SAND) at the beach now?

EXPAND: Do you say you notice the (WHITE or BLUE) of the waves the most?
Comment on student response.
EXPAND: Would you desire waves as (POWERFUL or RUSHING)?
Comment on student response.

MATH: If a wave hits the short every 5 seconds. How many times in a minute do waves crash against the shoreline? (11 or 12.)?

STATE: Many animals camouflage at the beach. White crabs on the beaches of Hawaii can be hard to see until you almost step on one.

ASK: What do some animals at the beach do? (CAMOUFLAGE. or FLAMBOYANTATING)?

EXPAND: Soldiers wear fabric that camouflages. Do you think camouflage means to (TIGHTEN or BLEND IN.)?
"Yes, blend in to surroundings."
MATH: There are 4 beaches with 25 crabs that camouflage on each. How many crabs are camouflaging? (100. or 120)?

STATE: It is amazing that much of the world's wildlife is found in the deep ocean. There are still animals we haven't discovered.

ASK: Much of the world's wildlife is found in the (RIVER or OCEAN.)?
"Most of the earth's crust is ocean."
EXPAND: What would be a large creature you find in the sea? (ELEPHANT or WHALE.)?
"Both the elephant and whales are mammals like you and me."
MATH: Soma rode on the back of the whale for 29 minutes. 13 of those minutes, she was up in the air on top of the water spout coming from the blow hole in the whale. How many minutes we she not on the water spout coming from the blow hole? (16. or 18)?
"That would be crazy. Do you think that is even possible? (YES or NO)?"

STATE: How you every noticed the abundance white bubbles. This is sea foam. Sometimes it can be fun experience the texture of it.

ASK: There is sea (FOAM. or MOISTURE) that I mentioned?

EXPAND: What word do you put with foam? (GRASS or BUBBLES.)?

EXPAND: Would you rather eat (SEAFOAM or KISS A CRAB)? ☺
"It is best you do neither. Both have bacteria on them that shouldn't be near the mouth!!"
MATH: Melissa kissed 15 sharks and Andres kissed 39 crabs. How many sea animals were kissed? (54. or 64)?

STATE: Many people associate the ocean or beach with relaxation and a break from the cares of life.

ASK: Mean people (RELINQUISH or ASSOCIATE.) the beach with relaxation?

EXPAND: To associate is to (CONNECT TO. or FORGET ABOUT)?

EXPAND: Write a sentence using the word 'relax.' (*If student is able, they should generate their own sentence, otherwise they can fill in the blanks for this one*) Popper (STOOD or SAT) on the (FOAM or BEACH) to (RELAX or DRAW).

MATH: If 35 people relaxed by the beach, but 12 of them were stung by a jelly fish, how many were not stung? (23. or 24)?

EXTENSION ACTIVITY: Have the student list five words that go with the beach (use choices if needed). Then have them create a story or sentences from those words. (use choices if needed).

LESSON 20: THE SKUNK

Main Cognitive Objective(s): Students will acquire knowledge and gain understanding of skunks

Application of Math: Math facts unrelated to the lesson

Materials: picture of a skunk, video of a skunk spraying

STATE: The skunk is black and white striped <u>mammal</u> belonging to the weasel family. It is about the size of a house cat. (*present a picture of a skunk and help the student look at it*)

ASK: A skunk is a (MAMMAL. or REPTILE)?

SPELL: Let's spell CAT.

MATH: 6x8= (45 or 48.)? And 7x4= (28. or 39)? Then, 25x3= (75. or 85)? (*Continue with more math facts if needed.*)

EXPAND: Do you think the skunk looks more like a (CAT or WEASEL)?
Comment on student's response.

STATE: When a skunk feels <u>threatened</u>, it stamps its front feet (*point out the front feet*) and raise its tail to warn it is going to <u>spray</u> its enemy.

ASK: The skunk stamps its (BACK or FRONT.) feet when it feels (WET or THREATENED.)?

MATH: 75/5= (15. or 17)? And 65/5= (13. or 16)? And 8/2= (4. or 6)?

EXPAND: If someone or something is threatened, they feel they will be (SAFE or HARMED.)?
"Yes, they will feel harmed."
EXPAND: Make a sentence with the word 'spray.' (*If a student is able to generate their own sentence, then they should do that, otherwise they can use choices*) <u>The </u>(GIRL or BOY) <u>took a </u>(SPRAY. or ELEPHANT) <u>bottle and </u>(SPRAYED or THREW) <u>it at the </u>(CHEETAH or MONKEY<u>).</u>

MATH: 45+53= (96 or 98.)? And 34+29= (63. or 73)? Then 89+26= (115. or 116)?

STATE: If the threat doesn't go away, the skunk will spray its enemy in the eyes with<u> two glands</u> at the bottom of its tail. (*Show short video clip if student is tolerating the lesson well*)

ASK: How many glands does it have? (2. or 3)?

EXPAND: When the skunk sprayed, it was (COOL or CREEPY)?
Comment on the student's response.
MATH: 47-29= (18. or 19)? And 58-23= (35. or 36)? And then 61-29= (31 or 32.)?

EXPAND: You have glands too. You can (SWEAT. or CAVITY) glands?
"Yes, sweat glands produce sweat to help regulate your body's temperature."

STATE: The spray stinks and the <u>foul smell</u> can remain for a number of days.

ASK: The smell is (OLD or FOUL.)?

EXPAND: Do you think you'd like to be sprayed by a skunk? (YES or NO)?
Comment on the student's response. Something like: "Most of us wouldn't, but if you like strong smells like poop, maybe you'd like the smell."
MATH: 32/2= (15 or 16.)? Does the problem 49/3 have a remainder? (YES. or NO)? And Does 18x2=36? (YES. or NO)?

EXPAND: Give me another definition of the meaning of foul? Does it have to do with (SPORTS. or COUNTING)?
"Yes, sports like a foul ball."

STATE: Skunks <u>prey</u> on small birds, eat bird <u>eggs</u>, small rodents, and some fruits.

ASK: A skunk might eat a small (CAT or BIRD.)?

EXPAND: Would you rather eat a (BIRD or CAT)?
Comment on student's response.
MATH: Is 68 (< or >.) than 67? And is 89 (<. or >) 100? Last, is 46 (< or =.) 46?

EXPAND: Would you be more likely to eat a (RODENT or FRUIT) if you were a skunk?
Comment on student's response. Maybe give your opinions.
SPELL: Spell EGGS.

EXPAND: 'Prey' is a homophone meaning it sounds like a different word that is spelled different and means something different. That word would be (PRAY. or PRIVATE)?
"Yes, this P-R-A-Y is connected to talking to God. The P-R-E-Y is connected to food an animal chases after to eat."
MATH: 35x2= (70. or 80)?

STATE: <u>Owls</u> prey on skunks. Scientist believe they are able to tolerate the smell of skunks because of their <u>poor </u>sense of smell.

ASK: The (WEASEL or OWL.) preys on skunks?

SPELL: Spell POOR.

ASK: The Owl has a (GOOD or POOR.) sense of smell?

MATH: 23+9= (32. or 42)? And 45+31= (76. or 84)?

EXPAND: Do you think a skunk would be tasty? (YEP or NOPE)?
Comment on the student's response.

EXTENSION ACTIVITY: Have the student tell their opinion of skunks. Then have them write a short summary. If the student needs to use choices, then use choices.

THE MATH GUY

When students are doing instinctual action and additionally are auditorily over stimulated (sometimes marked by laughing—not a happy laugh in reality—and sometimes can hardly perform) I observed Soma being very quiet and resorting to making a paper model of some figure. She quietly and carefully folds/ tapes the figure and involves the students in different aspects of the process. Slowly she increases their performance into spelling different parts of the body they create. When she does talk, it is extremely quiet and minimal.

From this, I got the idea of what I call the math guy. I do a similar thing, but I write on a piece of paper and hold up for the student to spell that says something like this: *"We are making a math guy."* I hope hold it up and make sure the student reads. Sometimes I take the student's finger and having the student point to each word. I keep the statements short since not all students have the visual tolerance to look at long statements. Then I start to make the math guy. Next, I write: *"Write a math problem on each body part."* I have the student read it the same way. Then after making a body part I will point to it and/ or write: *"First, let's put a math problem on his head."* Then I hold up the math stencil or numberboard and the student writes out a problem. I write the problem on the person's head. Once the student has the idea, I just point to the body part, then hold up the numbers for the student to create the math problem.

Next, I have the student go back through and solve all the math problems. See below for models of what it might look like in different phases of the process.

This task doesn't work (when doing silently and carefully folding) if the student needs auditory input and needs less visual input. For students needing auditory input, they need a bit more active pace with more back and forth exchanges.

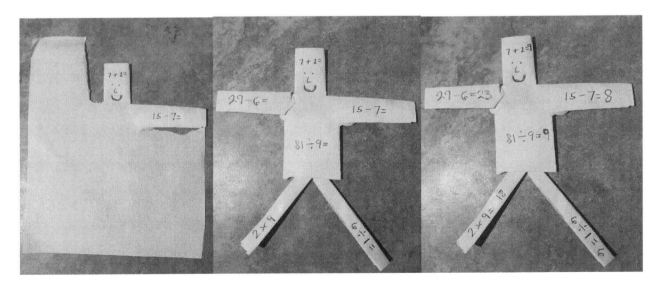

LESSON 21: DERINKUYU—UNDERGROUND CITY

> **Main Cognitive Objective(s):** Students will acquire knowledge and gain understanding of Derinkuyu, the underground city in Turkey.
>
> **Application of Math:** Begin with 'the Math Guy' then lead into the lesson putting math into the lesson at different points.
>
> **Materials:** Pictures of Derinkuyu. Tape and paper for the math guy. Map of Turkey and the surrounding areas
>
> SOURE: https://www.google.com/amp/s/www.history.com/.amp/news/8-mysterious-underground-cities

STATE: OK, now let's see…

Make the math guy as explained on the page before.

STATE: Now that we have made a math guy, perhaps he'd live in this city I heard about in <u>Turkey</u>.

ASK: Where would this math guy live perhaps? (GREECE or TURKEY.)?

EXPAND: (*hold up the map of Turkey*) Now we are looking at Turkey. Let's point to Turkey on the map. (*have the student point to Turkey*)
"Turkey is surround by a lot of water."

STATE: In Turkey, build in the <u>8th century</u> BC, the Hittites built an <u>underground</u> city called Derinkuyu.

ASK: Derinkuyu was an (UPPER or UNDERGROUND.) city?

EXPAND: Would you be able to see the city when standing on top of the ground? (NOPE. or SURE)?
"That's right, it is underground so the point is you can't see them. They are hidden."
MATH: 2x3= (4 or 6.)?

STATE: It served as a <u>refuge</u> in times of <u>war</u> or even invasions.

ASK: It was a refuge in times of (HOPE or WAR.)?

EXPAND: Would word would go with war? (EXPLOSION. or REGRESSION)?
"Yes, explosion, guns, hatred, cannon, sword, horse, army, etc."
MATH: If there were 9 explosions every hour for 3 hours, how many explosions altogether? (26 or 27.)?

EXPAND: If you are looking for a refuge, you'd be looking for say a (SAFE HAVEN. or PARK)?
"Everyone likes a place to feel safe. I feel safe in my home, or a church…"

STATE: The city was self-contained with 18 levels and could house 20,000 people.

ASK: So, how many stories were there? (18. or 20)? And there were 20,000 (COWS or PEOPLE.) that could live in it?
"So, one of the people could be our math guy if he lived back then."
EXPAND: Do you think that 18 stories is (TALL or SHORT)?
"That is a tall building. Most homes are 1 to 3 stories tall."
MATH: Derinkuyu has an earthquake. 5 of the 18 levels collapsed. How many are still in good shape? (13. or 15)?

EXPAND: Would you like to live there? (YES or NO)?
"Comment on the student's response."

STATE: It had wells, kitchens, oil presses, school rooms, bathrooms, and ventilations systems.

ASK: Let's name something that was found in Derinkuyu. Wouldyou say (VENTILATION SYSTEM. or TECHNOLOGY ROOM)?

EXPAND: You'd need ventilation for (MATH or FRESH AIR.)?
"Yes, because back then they had to cook over fires—no electricity like we use. And think about smell from bathrooms and breathing people."
MATH: 18/2= (8 or 9.)? And 16/8= (2. or 3)?

EXPAND: Do you think education is (IMPORTANT or WASTE OF TIME)?
Comment on student's response.

STATE: If there was a threat, they could seal off each level with a monolithic stone door.

ASK: They could seal off each level with a (SAND or MONOLITHIC.) door?

EXPAND: Monolithic is a big object make from on thing. So, the one non-cut item these doors were made out of was (STONE. or SAND)?
"Yes, it was made from one slab of stone."
MATH: Let's say each of the 18 levels had 2 monolithic doors. How many monolithic doors are there in Derinkuyu? (36. or 37)?

EXPAND: If you are threatened, someone wants to (HARM. or LOVE) you?
"Sometimes threats are real and some are imagined."

STATE: Eventually, Byzantine <u>Christians</u> inhabited it as can be seen by the frescos and <u>chapels</u>.

ASK: Evidence that Christians inhabited it are the frescos and (TENTS or CHAPELS.)?

EXPAND: Chapels goes with (FOE or GOD.)?
Comment on student's response.
MATH: A religious man worshiped for 18 minutes are Monday and 24 minutes on Tuesday. How many minutes altogether did he worship? (41 or 42.) minutes?

EXPAND: Christians, of course, believe in (CHRIST. or ANIMAL LEADERS)?
"Yes, they believe Christ is the Son of God and came to save the world from death and sin."

STATE: It was rediscovered in the <u>1960's</u> one a man came upon one of the tunnels <u>renovating</u> his house.

ASK: So, this place was rediscovered in (1960. or 1850)?

EXPAND: If you were renovating your house and saw a tunnel would you (SCREAM or EXPLORE)?
Comment on the student's reponse.
MATH: 22-2= (19 or 20.)?

EXTENSION ACTIVITY: Have the student write a short story on a day in the life of the math guy in Derinkuyu. Use choices if needed.

Printed in Great Britain
by Amazon